A

Production

To Contact Author or Publisher for bookings or questions please use the following mediums:

Website: www.blackevemedia.com

Email: Blackevemedia@gmail.com

Mail (address is exact): PO BOX 381135, Desoto TX 75138

Twitter: @BlackEveMedia

Instagram: blackevemedia

YouTube: BlackEve Media

#YBA

The 21st Century Guide to ~~Surviving~~ Thriving

Porscha Kelley, M.S.

BlackEve Media (Publishing Division)

Dallas, TX

Copyright © 2016 by DaPorscha Kelley

All rights reserved.

No part of this book may be reproduced in any form or by any means electronic, photocopying, recording, or otherwise, without permission in writing from the publisher, except by a reviewer who may quote brief passages in a review.

ISBN: 978-0-9971721-0-2

Library of Congress Control Number: 2016908408

This book is dedicated firstly to my nephew D'Andre and my two nieces Da'Mya and Jewelz.

And secondly to: Tamir Rice, Trayvon Martin, Freddie Grey, Sean Bell, Keith Childress, Bettie Jones, Kevin Matthews, Leroy Browning, Roy Nelson, Tiara Thomas, Cornelius Brown, Chandra Weaver, Richard Perkins, Michael Brown, Anthony Ashford, Rayshaun Cole, Junior Prosper, Keith McLeod, India Kager, Christian Taylor, Walter Scott, Lavall Hall, Jamie Croom, Monique Jenee Deckard, Naeschylus Vinzant, Andrew A. Williams, Ledarius Williams, Yvette Henderson, Thomas Allen Jr., Kendre Omari Alston, Brandon Jones, Ian Sherrod, Tiano Meton, Jermonte Fletcher, Darin Hutchins, Glenn C. Lewis, Kavonda Earl Payton, Donte Sowell, Natasha McKenna, Herbert Hill, Markell Atkins, Rodney Walker, Artago Damon Howard, Kevin Davis, Quentin Smith, Terrence Gilbert, Carlton Wayne Smith, Cameron Tillman, Warren Robinson, Rodney Hodge, ALTON STERLING, PHILANDO CASTILE ….. & the 500+ murdered this year. (I am you & you are me)

A Special "Thank You" to the following people:

K. Johnson

B. J. Talton

E. Victor

M. Ware

L. Caston

C. Andrews

Coach Carter

Professor James Small

*Truth Seeker. Nubian. Trill. Basic. Thug. Nappy & Happy. Oreo.
Crip. Tar Baby. Ratchet. Brilliant. Fly. High Yella. African. Bro.
Hopeless. Gifted. Unapologetic. Hood. Turn Up. Do It For the
Vine. Black Girl Magic. Dope Boy Fresh. Scholar. Ghetto.
Hustle. Black Power. Nigga-rigged. Creative. Invisible.
Criminal. Thot. It's Lit. Dab. Entrepreneur. My Nigga. Blood.
Stay on Fleek. Culture Vultures. Original. Throw Shade. Cocky.
YOLO. Nappy & Happy. Innovative. Hood. Nubian. Basic.
Nigga-rigged. High Yella. Thug. Oreo. Crip. Tar Baby. Ratchet.
Brilliant. African. Bro. Unapologetic. Hopeless. Gifted. Turn Up.
Black Girl Magic. Dope Boy Fresh. Scholar. Ghetto. Black
Power. Creative. Invisible. Trill. Criminal. Truth Seeker. Thot.
It's Lit. Dab. Entrepreneur. Fly. My Nigga. Blood. Stay on
Fleek. Culture Vultures. Original. Cocky. Throw Shade. YOLO.
Basic. Thug. Fly. Oreo. Crip. Tar Baby. Ratchet. Brilliant.
African. Bro. Hopeless. Trill. Gifted. Cocky. Turn Up. Black Girl
Magic. Nubian. Dope Boy Fresh. Scholar. Ghetto. Innovative.
Black Power. Hood. Creative. Hustle. Invisible. Nappy & Happy.
Criminal. Thot. It's Lit. Dab. Entrepreneur. My Nigga. Blood.
Stay on Fleek. Culture Vultures. Original. Throw Shade. Nigga-
rigged. YOLO. High Yella. Unapologetic. Truth Seeker. Basic.
Thug. Oreo. Crip. Tar Baby. Ratchet. Brilliant. African. Bro.
Hopeless. Gifted. Turn Up. Black Girl Magic. Nubian. Dope Boy
Fresh. Scholar. Ghetto. Black Power. Trill. Hustle. Creative.
Invisible. Criminal. Thot. It's Lit. Dab. Cocky. Entrepreneur. My
Nigga. Blood. Stay on Fleek. Culture Vultures. Fly. Original.
Nigga-rigged. Throw Shade. YOLO. Hood. Basic. Thug. Oreo.
Crip. Tar Baby. Innovative. Ratchet. Brilliant. African. Bro.
Hopeless. Cocky. Gifted. Nappy & Happy. Turn Up.
Unapologetic. Black Girl Magic. Nigga-rigged. Dope Boy Fresh.
Scholar. Ghetto. Black Power. High Yella. Creative. Invisible.
Criminal. Fly. Nubian. Thot. It's Lit. Dab. Entrepreneur. My
Nigga. Blood. Stay on Fleek. Culture Vultures. Original. Nappy.*

#YBA

YOUNG BLACK & AMERICAN

Table of Contents

Note to Reader:

This is a contemporary piece written not to the form of academic standards, but more so as a real conversation piece (an active conversation—contractions, Ebonics, and all) to evoke thought, promote a thorough observation, and prompt change achieved through action!

DISCLAIMER: Any and all suggestions in this book are not necessarily backed by substantial legal expertise. The author is not held liable for any financial, legal, occupational, or personal advice.

Introduction

To my #YBAs (Young Black Americans),

When I started this book, I went back and forth within myself trying to decipher how to disseminate this information in efforts to change both your mindset and actions. I couldn't decide whether it would be more effective to blow your mind by deprograming you first [Chapters 4-5]; or, to offer up direct advice regarding those early adulthood challenges that follow high school [Chapters 2-3].

Consider the following questions. As black youth in America today, what is your biggest fear, hope, dream, or hurdle? What are the hardest questions about yourself, your existence, your environment, and your reality that you feel no one can answer? When you look at your family and how you live, do you ever wonder if this is really what the future holds for you? Do you wonder how you can do better? Or, how in the hell your situation even got this way? All black people don't come from the jets (public housing or projects); so, why is your family still there...or just around the corner from them? Plenty of people go to college! Why is it that no one in your family has ever attended; and why is everyone all on your back to be the first to go?

You always see the "perfect" white family, with both parents in the household, three kids, and a dog. Does it make you wonder why your folks are separated or spending so much time in and out of jail? How will life be different for you? Is being an entertainer the only way to make it out the hood? Does that mean that you're screwed if you can't rap, sing, or dance that well; or if you just happen to be two feet and a couple of inches shy of fitting the mold of a professional athlete? These are all painstaking questions 1st generation game-changers pose to themselves while they struggle to transform their own lives, breaking their family's cycle of dysfunction. These are many of the same questions I posed to myself, and honestly, I have yet to answer them all.

So now you're probably thinking, "Well hell, I should just throw in the towel right now if there's no real solution to this generational-struggle." But there is hope yet!

I've found the two major keys to "winning" in the game of life:

1) Reject all the bullshit that society projects as an accomplishment in its entirety; and

2) Stop questioning whether your personal hardships are too difficult to overcome.

God gave you the resilience to overcome **everything** (evident in the fact that you continue to wake up day after day).

YOUR LIFE HAS PURPOSE!

Sincerely,

A black girl that has found her purpose

Chapter 1: Log on to WorldStar.com, the Modern Day Minstrel Show

My reason for writing this book is to help you fully recognize not the potential, but the evident part in you that has been hidden from you. This is the essence of your blackness that "they" want, but do not possess: the favor of GOD evident in our melanin, speech, dance, spirituality, and relentlessness in life. The purpose of this book is to promote growth at varying levels: factual, spiritual-self, mental, and intellectual; particularly for black teens of under-developed backgrounds. I have a particular affinity for this audience based upon my own upbringing and struggles while growing up in a single-parent, low-income household.

Looking back at those days, my surroundings and understanding (or what I thought was an understanding) of what a good life consisted of and how I thought I would ultimately get there, was very small and skewed. I thought like a poor person. As smart as everyone said I was, I still had a poor person's state-of-mind culturally, spiritually, and financially. I'm still in a growth phase; but today, I can say that I have a broader sense of reality and, more importantly, a deeper understanding of the false reality society dictated for me. My new found actuality has been based upon the dispelling of misconceptions and miseducation—both from my family's cyclical blindness and the public educational system's lack-luster political driven agenda.

Being #YBA (young, black, and American) honestly equates to an inherent struggle. But, let's be real. The "black struggle" is such a played out notion. Everybody's tired of hearing about it. Besides, "they" killed all our revolutionaries and bought-out those that carry the current black influence with million dollar contracts. Nobody's walking around in black leather carrying shotguns like the 60s. It's not like it used to be. Now don't get me wrong, the struggle is real, but the notion is an old one.

It is the subject that white people shy away from—rot with images of white masters lashing their black slave-property; heavy with generational curses passed down to (so called) wayward Millennials (you). It is the subject that we as African-Americans hang on to as the omnipresent stem of our setbacks. It is the subject that our other colored brothers and sisters—Mexican Americans, Asian Americans, Middle Eastern Americans, etc., feel overshadowed by, because they believe that it is time for their struggle to be heard and explored to the same depths as the black struggle. It is a subject that is so deeply intertwined in American history that it is synonymous with all the major milestones of the American story from onset to current times.

Time and time again, black society in America has examined the black struggle but has come up with no distinct answer as to why the struggle still exists. Why do we still insist that the black struggle exists in a day when America has its first African American President? The concept sounds too ridiculous to even have to say out loud; America has a black President, yet the black struggle still persists and is no doubt worsening.

The current surge of publicized black on black crime continues to worsen—especially in the upper part of Chicago (nicknamed Chi-RAQ) with rates equaling and then surpassing war rates of death in Afghanistan and Iraq. [A decade from now the government will probably formally apologize for dropping off crates filled with automatic weapons supplying misguided black youth with means to exterminate each other and giving reason for underfunding the public school system. This will clear the way for gentrification in the form of foreigners invading and controlling pass predominate urban meccas.] The continuous surge of white on black crime grows more and more blatant with hundreds of Trayvon Martin-like cases in the news everyday—where white gunmen are found innocent in court and black childless mothers are offered millions of dollars in hush money behind the scenes.

The most pressing issue within the current struggle is OUR black kids; YOU! The growth and survival tactics that the last generations weren't able to pass down to you are now the things that you have to take the time to learn and further cultivate for yourselves. In particular, as a disadvantaged black teen, real talk needs to be at the center of your maturation: a sense of self-knowledge, a sense of financial responsibility, a broader sense of culture, and the expulsion of fruitless traditional group-think. Honestly, our community has failed you; and it's time to pick up the pieces. This process begins with knowing one's self and feeling out the next steps in your life through knowledgeable decisions; not cookie-cutter life plans that everyone has carved out for you.

The onset of my own consciousness took place in grad school. In particular, an eye-opening experience occurred in a course titled *Diversity in Criminal Justice*. Somehow or another, during one of our class discussions, we got on the subject of roots and self-identification. I was one of two black women in a room full of 20 or so white people—no excuse me, Scottish, Spaniards, and Jewish individuals. You see, once the door flew open for them to express their family tree, everybody in that room was more than able to identify themselves and distinguish their families' origin far beyond these "United States." I remember one guy talking about his Scottish roots in detail; dating the exact years his family arrived here.

After a good portion of the class divulged their family histories, I raised my hand. That angry black woman was about to come out and make everybody feel uncomfortable. I addressed the entire class and proclaimed that their histories and family identities meant nothing to me. It meant nothing to me because I didn't have one. It was stolen from me. It was partly my jealousy speaking because I didn't have one to speak of; and they did. I found that this lack of self-knowledge not only excluded me from the conversation; but, from having true connections in this world.

So many times, as black kids, we are surrounded by people so much like ourselves that we don't even realize that we are missing a part of ourselves (family and cultural history). We almost all (as black people) are in the same situation. I didn't fully realize this until I was sitting in this class with these "cultured" people. And when I say cultured, I mean cultured within themselves. Many of them weren't well traveled or bilingual, but they knew their family histories and the countries from which they originated.

I had nothing to help ground me; nor did I see how I fit into the puzzle of America, or world history, for that matter…except for the fact that I was black. I knew at some point somebody in my family was a slave; and the golden stories of "Indian in our family" existed to explain away the light, bright and almost white great-great grandmother I knew and loved. The sad part was that I was 22 years old, pretty well educated and I knew absolutely nothing about myself and how the world outside of my own little "black-hole" operated. All I knew was black people—my people—were survivors! But, I knew nothing about how deep those ties were; as I saw none of our history.

I took on a personal responsibility in writing this book in order to further inspire the growth (spiritual and self-conscious) of the next little black girl and boy lost in the web of lies and disillusion of this misguided world. I recognize that you are overcome by the superficial lies and illusions in mainstream media because all day long the message of "nothingness" is pushed down your throat.

Through TV and poorly written history books you are subconsciously taught:

1) Black people didn't exist or do anything worth noting until slavery

2) Assimilating into white culture is the only road to societal acceptance and achievement

3) Black culture is synonymous with being ghetto and lacking civility.

Even now in 2016, many in the black community lament the exit of Barak Obama thinking he was the 1st and only black president of America; when in reality he's probably like the 9th black President [Google "America's Black Presidents" and see what I'm talking about]. It's time to wash away the mentality you've been so coached in—the whitewashing of your mind and ambitions. It's time to stop aspiring to be the first black such-and-such, to step into the reality that we did everything first; and to realize whatever we did second, we did it better and, that you can be the next **great** such-and-such!

You must realize that nothing exists without black-ness. The words in this book could not express ideas if it were not colored. God created light **from the darkness**. The human race stems from that of a black man and woman (scientifically proven, even National Geographic concurs)! We, black and colored people alike, resemble the original idea of man; and, we still to this day hold within us something that they (white people/the other) cannot fully understand, comprehend, or emulate.

Today, black culture is extremely popular. Especially during the era of the proverbial "turn-up"; as it's considered fun, entertaining, and cool to exhibit "black behavior." The problem with this is that for those of us who are "inconveniently black" during times of crisis or injustice, the battle is getting way too out of hand. Our culture continues to be bought and sold; then used against us to perpetuate a stereotype that demonizes us through various streams of propaganda (like super ratchet reality shows). This makes it easier to dehumanize us and abuse us politically, financially, and physically (as in unjustified police brutality). But let's be real. Is this anything new to us; as in a shocking phenomenon? The saddening and readily apparent answer is, no. In your mama's voice, "Hell Na'll!"

The manner and rate in which your self-worth and potential ability as a black youth is being purged from you is so alarming. They coming at y'all hard! (When I say "they" I don't mean white people in general. I'm referring to the elusive system of racial discrimination; and not so much the bigots of today that outright exude hatred. I explain this concept more in chapter 2 and revisit it in chapter 4.) The main message to my little black brothers and sisters is that, if at any time in your life you allow someone to define the reflection of who you think you are, then HE WILL! For hundreds of years, systematic racism has done that; with the help of some bigots and a well-perpetuated unjust legal system. It has shaped our opinion of ourselves so much so that we as black people have lost a bit of who we really are underneath all the levels of stereotypical bullshit. This campaign has grown even stronger through the use of reality TV and social media (mainly because of their viral nature).

False examples of what represents blackness are placed on these superficial platforms and the cheap and faulty version of who we are as black people is rendered unto the world. Today, our black culture is no exception. "Coonery-and-Buffoonery" as Spike Lee would put it, is for sale and exploitation. We, as black people, have lost our own culture and have adapted some bastardized version that white America uses as entertainment, continues to sensationalize, and perpetuates as truth. The same elusive system of racial discrimination has used this image to define us as separate and definitely not equal to "them." We went from being that **N-e-g-g-u-r** to being a Nigger (a reference I will further explain in Chapter 5). Worst yet, we have played into some Ponzi scheme; having begun to believe and willingly exhibit the falsehood of these same bastardized images.

Now before you close this book; or, get ready to fire up a WorldStar video on your phone while assuming I'm about to get into some rant about the "Evil White Man" as the devilish slave master, pump your brakes. One thing I will not do in this book is dwell on slavery! I chose not to do this for a few reasons:

- First, it points a finger (not saying that there isn't a finger to be pointed), and we are so far gone from that yielding any results to our holistic situation. It would render no benefit to brood over this subject until we establish some basis and context.

- Second, as we continue to look at slavery as the root cause of black folk's dysfunction, for some reason, it has become our starting point of reference of our history, which is far from the truth of who we really are as black people. It falsely begins to trump our true origin as the father and mother of mankind—the original people God placed on earth.

o Thirdly, diverting focus off of slavery should allow us to focus on the picture at large; further focusing on a true solution to our community woes versus pinpointing just one of the multi-faceted causes of our collective dysfunction.

So why did I reference WorldStar.com in the chapter heading? Now, I know that for many of you, WorldStar is the go to site for quick ratchet entertainment. It's a place to laugh at someone else's expense, catch the latest celebrity dirt; or, to see a hood fight without being within dangerous proximity. But at some point, don't you catch yourself thinking, "Damn, my people need to do better." We seem to still be putting on a minstrel show for the world to view; and posts "likes." We are still repeating a disparaging history.

Minstrel show: a U.S. form of entertainment developed in the 19th century of comic skits, variety acts, dancing, and music, performed by white people in blackface or, especially after the U.S. civil War, by black people.

-Wikipedia definition

Youtube "Minstrel show" (look for both black and white actors in "black face")

The minstrel show was the degradation of black people on the Hollywood stage. It was drenched in "shucking and jiving"; ladled over stereotypical ideologies and disparaging depictions of African-Americans. Initially, white people would dress in black-face and make fun of the way they thought we as black people talked (with a twang they would get lost in), walked (with swag they never could imitate), danced (with soul they couldn't duplicate); and the manner in which we interacted with each other. This became the dominate form of entertainment; especially down south.

White people controlled, and further disparaged, the image of the black Americans through media like this so much so that eventually; these were the only type of roles that talented black actors could get once the doors to the bigger stages of show business were open to blacks. White media proscribed the manner in which we portrayed ourselves on film; and through entertainment, they were able to control the way everyone else viewed us and our persona. Black actors were mostly caste as buffoons, maid-servants, over-sexualized animalistic beings, and the like. This thereby cultivated our false stigmas. It's a little disheartening to admit that not much has changed in the past 100 years or so in reference to the images or ideas reflected in the classical minstrels and the current portrayal of black people in the media.

You're probably thinking, "What does any of this have to do with black people, especially #YBAs today?"

How many times do you turn on the TV and go straight to the newest reality show, i.e., Love and Hip Hop, the Real Housewives, the Pastors of LA, the Women of Medicine, the Bad Girls Club or Keeping up with the Kardashians (I almost threw up writing down the last one)?

[Disclaimer: I am far from holier-than-thou, because I do partake in a housewife show or LHH here and there; but I starkly understand what is being thrown at me.]

Anyway, my point is that what you watch on a consistent basis affects what you think is normal; or acceptable, and we all know that the ratchet stuff that goes down on these shows are anything but acceptable in the real world. This is especially true, being a black person, that the cops are **more than willing** to shoot down in the street in order to receive a multi-million dollar book deal (coined by Darren Wilson—murderer of Mike Brown).

Every time you visit WorldStar or Media Takeout to get your dose of "black entertainment," you open yourself up to a vision of false impressions. You better believe that the people on these shows are getting paid to act an ass **on camera**. The scenes they shoot are planned—that's usually why nobody goes to jail after a physical altercation; and if they do, they are released because they have signed an agreement not to really press charges against cast mates.

Reality TV is about as real as a front-lace. But what "they" are getting you to do is waste your precious time watching the foolishness; in which some of you actually get emotionally involved tweeting after every show. This is time you can be spending making money on a job or figuring out how to make money on your own as an entrepreneur. And those of you who are really getting taken advantage of really believe the ways of "reality life" and have started actually imitating reality TV activities such as fights on the school yard, or in the club so others can post them on social media, or, recorded sexual acts that will surely embarrass you later down the line (and in many cases can count as a felony in some states even if it's minor to minor sexting and/or acts).

Sometimes fun isn't just fun, and some things you do for the Vine can resemble the old school minstrel acts; especially when some black kids thought it was cool to get in the bathtub and set themselves on fire with rubbing alcohol ☺. I mean really. Not only did all of them make a fool of themselves, but a couple of them gave back to the medical system and surely pissed their parents off when they had to be admitted to the hospital for 3rd degree burns to their chest and private area. Just dumb asses! But you'll do anything for a "like" right? GTFOH! Don't resort to "coonery and buffoonery" it's a waste of time.

Stuntin': Everythang Stay on Fleek

Sound Track: Lost Kings by Jarren Benton (on Sound Cloud or YouTube)

There exists another aspect of "cooning" for a minstrel show—the costume. The costume and makeup that went into the production of a show were elaborate—complete grease paint, shiny suits, and outlandish wigs. Sound familiar?

Have you ever just people-watched, in particular—mixed company: white, black, and other (Mexican, Asian, etc.)? As black people, we usually standout! We can flex hard when it's time to dress for the occasion. I mean, it usually never fails. You can always find the brother with the shiny suit, the black woman with the obnoxiously huge hair; or, the cleanest Negro in the room (loudly matching brand name from head to toe).

See, my mama always told me that you shouldn't look like your struggle. She taught me how to maintain a decent well-kept appearance even if I was dead broke and had to get my "new" fit from the thrift store (before Maclemore made it cool); or, a garage sale. She also let me know that the person that's all out stuntin' is most probably doing worse than you would think. As I got older, I started to fully understand just what she was preaching.

When I was a kid, I didn't know what "struggling" meant. I knew what bills were; and, I knew that my brothers and I couldn't get certain toys, shoes, and clothes because they were too expensive. I also knew that we were provided for; but didn't necessarily have everything other kids had in a two parent household. By the time I got to high school (or should I say the "fashion show"), I saw what a "struggle" was by comparison! See, by this point, the microcosm of high school has or will weed you out and categorize you. As a black high school student, you either fall in one of a couple of groups: the "famed athlete", the "really smart kid", a "have," or a "have-not" (in addition to various other cliques that fall somewhere in between).

Lucky for me, I knew a lot of the answers in class and could help those in the "athletic" and "haves" category, so no one really picked on me for being a "have-not." By being a "have-not,"—meaning I "have-not" the latest J's; nor clothes, nor could I afford to get my hair done on a regular basis (you know all the things that are deathly important in high school). I ran the risk of being made fun of. To keep it 100, my family didn't even have a car. Our lights were cut off on the regular— despite my mother's best efforts. The water got cut off in rotation with the lights; sometimes, simultaneously.

I knew that my mother was stressed the hell out on a regular basis! But at school, nobody else seemed to have these same problems. At least, that's what I thought. It seemed like everybody came to school with brand name this and that. Didn't look like anybody else was struggling to me. I'm here to tell you that I wasn't the only one; and **you** aren't the only one.

It was hard maneuvering the social caste-system of high school when your situation has you at the bottom of the totem pole. But retrospect, coupled with Facebook, Instagram, etc., allows you to see that the stunnas usually end up at the bottom of the social ladder later on in life; but continue to floss for the audience.

As a whole, we as a people are still struggling. We are struggling financially, educationally, spiritually, and holistically. But we damn-sho try to compensate for it; unfortunately in the wrong way. Many of our familial situations are complicated by single-parent homes, CPS intervention, having parents in jail, teen pregnancy, grandmothers raising kids; and/or households living under the poverty line. Collectively, our black economics are looking bleak: high unemployment rates, a lack of black business owners and the availability of resources, black consumerism vs. owner/investor interests, our replication of the black $, the percentage of black prison population and how they charge us ridiculous premiums for calls and commissary. Black health issues continue to balloon; with certain diseases that affect us the most. I can write four or five books on the above problems; that's how deep-seeded our issues are.

Yeah, our President is black, but our struggle is still real; despite how well we stunt and try to hide it. As black people, we are just surviving; as we stay in the act of survival versus the act of thriving. Why? The truth is, by the time you reach adulthood, those categories of an average black high school student don't really change much. You either work for minimum wage; but dress like a million dollars, have a decent middle class job; but spend additional income to acquire more debt, join various high society leagues to match your professional occupation, or, you make your money off of putting your talent on the main stage and further promote the spending of black dollars on material things through your media persona (actors, athletes, entertainers, and the like).

We put on a front for everybody else for the sake of not being called out on other matters.

This type of behavior occurs on two main accords:

1) We show out amongst ourselves (competing with each other on a materialistic level)

2) a few of us (the "elite") try to fit the white-mold (completely subscribing to the standards/criticism of white America) in order to rest in circles of affluence.

Case #1 occurs in both the lower and upper financial rungs of the black community. Who has the newest pair of J's, Michael Kors bag, BMW, Audi, or the longest, most expensive bundle (the new "gold" of the hairweave world)? It doesn't matter if you are in the projects or the suburbs, these things seem to be of the utmost concern. The ones that rock these fads 1st gain the award of black admiration and envy; until the next person comes along with that "new-new," SMH ☺—and the cycle never ends because we continue to pass it to our children.

Because we all know that we don't shop "black-owned" businesses consistently, what do we gain from doing this? Our overzealous consumerism only benefits white corporate America—white fashion designers, foreign car companies, and Asian owned beauty suppliers [watch Chris Rock's *Good Hair* documentary if you really want to know how you got that 22"]. And let me stop you before you get to the great black entrepreneur Michael Jordan. How many black political issues has he stood behind? How many schools or parks has he built in your hood? There are more black owned and operated brands that could use our collective support.

My point is that our over emphasis on showing off for each other via consumerism doesn't replicate money in our community; nor does it promote growth or improve relations amongst us. The competition between ourselves use to be about educational and entrepreneurial advancement. But, I guess it's easier to slave at a minimum wage job in order to spend the whole check on shoes, hair, and jewelry just to be able to disparage the next black person and feel better about one's self. It reminds me of the House-Nigger/Field-Nigger quibble, "look at what Masta' just gave me."

Now let's look at the second behavior I described. Case #2 looks specifically at the black community that "made it," never looked back; and only associated with the other side. In other words, "if it ain't white, it ain't right." A certain appearance has to be maintained in order to be accepted by white people; and everything is done to disassociate themselves with black culture and their African roots.

This is stuntin' to a whole other degree; but it seems to be really popular these days. For example, you got Raven Symone and Whoopie Goldberg screaming on daytime TV that they are American—forget the African identifier. Stacey Dash makes the dumb ass comment that we shouldn't have a black history month or black TV stations like BET or TV One. You have the infamous black male that only associates with or marries white women once they "make it" (I don't have to list any names—just pick one). You have those that have come up from the bottom of the middle class, act as if they are disgusted by the "ghetto" and the "ratchet"; but have an uncle in the state penitentiary for selling that work on the corner. And all I can do is give the Kanye shrug.

As black people we have made it hard on each other to feel accepted. Either you're not black enough; or, you're too black [watch the movies *School Dazes* and *Dear White People*]. We exclude and ostracize ourselves because we have been tainted and afflicted by this standard of "whiteness" and what "they" have deemed important. Instead of us black people adapting and cultivating our own commutative levels of standards based securely on African principles, we have fully taken on a dysfunctional Westernized version of the "freed slave." Going forward, we should look at the basis of creating our own standards. Individually, people who live by their own standards are usually outcasts. But there is a sense of confidence and knowledge of self that it takes to be an actual individual, not a follower.

Watch classic movie *Bamboozled* (A Spike Lee Film)

One of the greatest progressions we as American black people have had, occurred during the Reconstruction period; up until the 1950s. The progress we made **on our own**—meaning excluding the worry of mixing into "dominant culture"—was momentous. [Please further research the work of W. E. B. DuBois and black Wall-Street in Tulsa Oklahoma.] We had our own high societies, banks, bus and car manufacturing companies, schools, theaters, and grocery stores.

We are and always have been able to hold our own; as there really is no need to try and fit a mold we aren't built to fit. **Be black, be innovative, and be accepting of one's self while respecting others; everything else will fall into place.**

In the show *Empire,* directed by Lee Daniels, one of the main characters, Andre, was trying to gain acceptance by both his family and society at large. He attempted to do this by going to bat for the family business, getting an Ivy-league education; and, by marrying a white woman. His father told him he will never be accepted by society because of his wife. He is still black. We all know what that means.

There are just certain places we will not be readily welcomed. But, should we even care? Why would you want to be "accepted" on a marginal basis somewhere when "they" don't really want you there? For example, I applaud the black 4-star recruit Jean Delance from Mesquite, TX who de-committed from OU after the SAE "nigger-rant" incident [Google full story]. He hit them where they could feel it, in their pockets. Black college athletes bring so much money and attention to schools. Another black athlete at the same school went on a viral rant about how he was tired of the racism on campus; and how they use the black men as race horses in sports. The school ended up making him apologize for his comments; while the white fraternity member who led the "nigger song" on the fraternity bus received a security guard on campus because he got threats☺. Imagine if more black athletes would step up and refuse to play for discriminating schools (which they have been). How much more respect would a university have to show to the black community?

Now some black people may say that this is just how the world works; and this is just how you have to play the game. Well, my question is why not be a game changer? Right now, we as black people are just surviving! 40 plus years later, and the theme song to the show *Good Times* still rings true when it points out that our main concern is just to "keep our heads above water." But, if we could stop trying to fit a mold strong held by white culture—a faction that will never fully accept us as we are; then, we can build a stronger black community by setting standards and positive goals for ourselves.

It's time to stop trying to over compensate for our struggle and start investing in solid values—building true education (not that Nazi-concentration version served up in most public schools), reestablish community relations, and strengthen black economics (restoring meaningful buying power and financial institutions). All this has to start with you.

If you let go of the idea of frivolous material items and recognize **planned obsolesce** [Google definition] for what it really is—a great marketing ploy, you will save yourself thousands of dollars and gain a deeper focus far beyond the common population. You can then concentrate on solving the pressing issues within your own family. Saving black America starts one household at a time.

Lost Ones, Bought Ones… Still Leased

A found soul amongst my lost people

Small and fickle minds: elevation needed.

They paralyzed you through lack of education—education of self

Misguided, destitute so you turned prostitute: money, clothes, alcohol, prestige, status, greed

You fall prostrate to a god that reflects them in their eyes

So oblivious of the blood of the Divine in your own likeness— MY GOD!

Our own power devoid,

Buried in the race for the American Lie- sorry I mean dream:

"Nigga be all you can be so you can give it to me"

—Uncle Sam

No Uncle Tom's Cabin here

Our community broken for the sense of "me"…"mine"… "I"… nigga… no "we"

Die said "Master"… Dead, you died. To yourself dead—MY GOD, RESURRECT!

Broken, used, and maneuvered: a pawn

Their rules dictate, while you die.

You wait,

You're shot, you wait...

No justice!

-None for you my nigga, wasn't made for you in the first place,

But you thought... No you bought the LIE!

JUST CONTINUE EATING YOUR PIECE OF THE
AMERICAN PIE

That EmptYness

We force feed 'em a lifestyle of impressions.

That fluff: that sugar-water & Kool-Aid when they need milk,

Then we turn around and expect gold from them when they
consume lyes and emptYness.

No substance, no culture, no history.

All homogeneous, no individuality, but they trying so hard.

Trying so hard to be free, but they don't know how; they don't
know who to be.

Their individuality is expressed through clothes with somebody
else's name on them. Shoes that costs as much as the library of
books that could have enlightened them.

Where's the sense of family?

The sense of worth?

The pride in having knowledge. For they are empty and thirsting
for attention.

They don't know Big Mama, ain't got no daddy, have no roots—
it's gonna be hell to bare any fruit.

Following the lost wondering why they ain't got nowhere—blind
leading the blind.

But honestly who can they even look up to, where are all the role
models?

When they die who is replacing them?

Eartha Kitt dies, Amber Rose gets her shine;

Mya Angelou dies, Kylie Jenner is the trending topic;

Nelson Mandela dies, Wayne and Baby's beef is up on the retweet

We empty y'all, and we need substance.

On to the Next

Soundtrack for this chapter: "Love Yourz" by J. Cole

I heard this message listening to the *Steve Harvey Morning Radio Show*: "Turn your excuse for not doing into your reason for doing and achieving!" As black youth, you may feel that you have so many barriers in front of you. But, those things should be the very reason to grind even harder and smarter. I know this firsthand; as I have felt like a freaking brick wall was in front of me as I got through high school. I was so scared to leave high school because I didn't truly see what was next. I just thought that as long as I didn't get pregnant early, I should be alright. I didn't see a clear path.

I was a decent student (A's and B's); so teachers and counselors pushed for me to attend college. But, I wasn't familiar with the process—real talk, I SERIOUSLY didn't think college was an option. **I didn't have any $$$$!** My junior year, I was like, "I might have to go to DeVry part-time and just work a regular little job." (Now this was before DeVry offered such a diversified program).

I was about to graduate 3rd in my class and had no particular focus or dream. It wasn't like I didn't care or wasn't concerned—I absolutely cared about my future, I just didn't completely understand how big and bright my future could be. This was because I was in this "I'm poor and black and focused solely on surviving" mindset. Like most of our households, I couldn't see past the next coming eviction or termination notice.

My visibility was really low and everything past graduation was real foggy. I didn't have anything in particular in my head like "I'm going to be a doctor, lawyer, teacher, or whatever'; as it didn't matter as long as I could support myself (survive). I was fine with just existing versus living. I was going to go to DeVry or ITT tech and be able to work on AC units; or, maybe venture into technical support (I knew they made "good money")! I had no time to dream; or to focus on a passion because of the struggle and the burden of worrying about surviving and paying bills.

I'm here to tell you that that is not the way to live, no matter what situation you were born into or what you may face today. The key is YOU. You have to be willing to move on to the next level. The way in which you choose to do so is your choice; just as long as you make up your mind to move! As black kids (from single-parent, financially unstable homes, a product of the foster care system, or whatever your particular situation may be) you are coached into the thought that you have very few options to "make it." A part of that reasoning exists because you probably know nothing else to aspire to; as your view is so limited. That mindset is not a result of your parents or family necessarily; but your environment, situation, and lack of access maintained through "the system." This just means that you have to try extra hard to construct some sort of internal vision of what is possible—you know, that stuff that well-to-do white, Asian, and even a minority of well-to-do black kids have access to (financial stability and the mind frame to grow and maintain actual wealth and gain culture).

At 28 years old, I can finally say that I am actually starting to come into that mindset. I've started focusing again; even dreaming a little more. As late as I feel that this has occurred, I know there are individuals like myself that I grew up with who haven't (and sadly probably will never) evolve because of a lack of exposure, a closed-mind, and the end result of "the system" consistently beating them down.

I want you—the "poor disenfranchised black kid"—to overcome all of the mental, physical, and spiritual roadblocks. I want to give you a heads up on some knowledge that I wish I could have accumulated earlier in my teenage years. For some reason, our community has missed passing along some basic pearls of wisdom. I could have been so much further by now with this information! But if you start today, you can go much further than myself; and then, pick up another younger person and help them along—replicating a positive cycle.

First, shed that negative stigma instilled within your family (by drug abusing parents, an absent father/mother, the lack of education, the lack of capital [$, land, and resources], etc.). Reconcile issues with your parents or caregivers. A lot of times when a terminal relationship exists between you and your parents, **it's because your parents are transposing their issues unto you**—I had the same type of situation happen to me.

The relationship between my mother and I went up and down for years because of the dysfunction she experienced between her and my grandmother (and probably a whole lot of other issues I know nothing about). You have to throw off those shackles. You are not your parents and should not have to bear their struggles or unresolved issues. Remember, no matter how much you do for someone it will never be enough! Do for yourself first, **emotionally** and **financially,** because who will you be able to turn to when you need help? If that answer is slim to none; then, you need to start investing more into the person you can depend on—yourself!

In order to begin healing these relationships you might need to seek counseling (either with that person or through independent sessions). This can be in a formal sense; as in a licensed professional you relate to, or, by just finding a mentor that has been in a similar situation. For some reason in the black community, we look at counseling in some negative light. We put up the bravado that we are "too strong for counseling" and only weak people go do "that."

Going to counseling doesn't mean you're crazy. It's a way to constructively resolve issues that may be deep-seeded. Obtaining another point of view can be hard to swallow, eye-opening, and monumental in your growth. Again, this doesn't have to be a clinical high priced situation. It can be as simple as joining the Big Brothers/ Big Sisters Program; or, finding a slightly older black mentor. Finding someone you actually vibe with or have a trust in is very important. This person may be the same race, sex, and/or have some of the same interests as yourself.

There are some things you are experiencing at this time that you know aren't right. There are some scars you are receiving right now via your parents, grand-parents, siblings; or, whomever, and it has come in the form of physical, verbal, mental, and/or another form of abuse. The number one thing to realize is that the person that hurt you (or is still hurting you) has the problem.

For your sake, you can't allow them to transfer that problem unto you. If you do; then it might cause you to internalize it and it becomes a problem in **your** life. Personally, that was the hardest thing to realize and work through; especially when that type of hurt comes from someone whom you're so closely connected, like family members. In order to setup a better life for yourself, you are going to have to step out of the victim's shoes, permanently. It's time to be proactive. What happened to you in the past doesn't matter so much because to a certain extent, you probably had no control over the situation. Today is a different day!

Once you commit to your self-healing process, the next step is to start evaluating your surroundings. The very people you allow into your life are the people that can hurt you the most. Watch who you hang around. Do you trust those around you; and, are they forward thinking individuals? Are they holding you back in some way? You should construct some kind of personal vetting system where you audition your current and possible friends. Yes I said audition! After all, it should be an honor to be associated with you, right? Doing this could help you weed out the snakes early on.

Chapter Notes:

_____

_____

_____

_____

_____

_____

_____

_____

_____

_____

_____

Chapter 2: Doing Better than Mama and Daddy

The ultimate goal is to advance and grow; generation by generation. For this to happen, an expansion of thinking and experience has to occur! Chapter 2 exposes you to your limitless future. It will shed light on possibilities I wish someone would have let me in on when I was in high school and college. The purpose of this chapter is to show a lane where you can thrive; and not just survive.

Graduation Fast Approaching:

So let's get real. Life ain't a game after high school. You will either end up wasting time (spending unnecessary $, relationship jumping, getting meaningless job after job, etc.); or, making the best of it (gaining knowledge, building wealth through sound financial practices, establishing a solid community through functioning relationships, etc.). If you get out here without some kind of plan, you will find yourself getting caught up in some foolishness. Even if you're not sure if you're going to college after high school, there are some things that you should definitely do by the time you graduate to set yourself up to be independent and productive.

Below is a list of affairs that should be prioritized right before you graduate from high school and get out into the real world. If your already in the real world and haven't dealt with some of these tasks; then you may want to jump on it. (Some items in this list should probably be re-evaluated every year; especially before college graduation.)

- By the end of your sophomore year in high school, you should know who your counselor is and set up a meeting with him/her to make sure you are on course to graduate. You should discuss your ranking in your class; as well as plans you may need to implement to move up in rank and prepare for post-graduation. Start investigating potential majors that appeal to you; or, start with careers that peak your interest and research the majors and certifications it takes to get into that profession.

- Start applying for scholarships (I don't care if you're a freshmen in high school and you're not even sure you want to go to college). You can start applying as early as 10 years old for certain scholarships. So yes, you are behind if you have not applied to at least 1 scholarship already. (I applied to my first scholarship in 7th grade. I didn't get it; but, I got in the practice of filling out the application and seeing exactly what scholarship committees are looking for.)

- Start going to summer school. Some junior colleges in your area will let you go to entry-level college classes and gain college credit at 14 and 15 years old. You could enter college as a sophomore or a junior by the time you graduate from high school. I wish I had known about this option because you save thousands of dollars by attending community college for basic level courses. To learn more information about this, visit the nearest **accredited** junior college and speak with an admissions counselor. [Google the story of Grace Bush from Florida, a 16-year-old black girl who graduated from high school and college at the same time.]

- If you are a college-bound senior, apply for early admission for all your prospective schools (for some, this may mean that you HAVE to start saving some amount of cash as early as your sophomore year for application fees in order to be ready to apply to schools). Some kids may qualify for vouchers that will take care of your application fees based on your family income. Please talk to your high school counselor and the college admissions counselors at your schools of choice.

- **$$$** Open a bank account; if you don't already have one. If you are opening your first account, a credit union may be a better fit because of the lack of fees and the smaller amount required to start the account. (You can open an account for as little as $5 at some credit unions.) With the way commerce is done today you will need to have a card secured by a financial institution; as the Rush card, the Walmart money card, and others like the ones you see on the commercials won't cut it all the time.

- **$$$** Learn and put into practice some financial discipline. Start saving some money for post-graduation. This can be for college books (if you're planning to continue school), gas/bus fare to get back and forth to work (I don't care if you don't have a job now, think forward and prepare for the future), for an apartment if you're in a situation where you have to move out upon graduation, or just in case of a basic emergency, etc.

- **$$$** Open a secure credit card with a credit union. A traditional credit card can be opened at a bank as well; but at the credit union your credit limit will be backed by the savings you have established, so over spending is harder to do. With the traditional card, your credit limit isn't backed by anything. If you are already pretty smart with your money and feel responsible enough to open a bank credit card, then go for it; but be cautious of monthly balances. [Google the difference between a secure and a credit card.]

- **$$$** CHECK YOUR CREDIT REPORT FOR ANY FOUL PLAY [log on to www.annualcreditreport.com]. If you do find some crazy activity on your credit report, 9 times out of 10 it probably will be the result of a family member who opened a phone, utility, or store account in your name. Just relax, you can dispute the charges; especially if you were under age at the time of the charge(s). Contact the people at the bottom of the credit report and let them know that you just became aware of the discrepancy and follow their instructions [see "Ca$h and Your Ratchet Priorities" for detail information].

- Insure that you have sufficient state ID and; or, driver's license and that it is not expired. If you have the money to do so, go ahead and get a passport book (they run about $175); or, a passport card (about $100). They are valid for 10 years; that's like $17.50/$10 a year. This will give you the ability to travel **when** the opportunity presents itself. I know people in their 20s, 30s, and 40s that don't have a passport. They claim they want to go on vacation or explore outside of their area code but don't even have the proper ID to do so. What do you think their chances are of actually going somewhere? Little to none. You're more likely to travel if you actually have the ID to do so.

- **$$$** Set up a budget, a savings goal, and an emergency plan in accordance to your current situation. Keep a calendar of your bills and literally write down when each bill is due and will be withdrawn (if you can, setup auto draft) In addition, periodically check your spending habits and how it effects your savings and checking account. How many times do you eat out or go on a sporadic shopping spree? Do you even have money in your savings? It may be time to check some bad habits.

- If you have a job evaluate your current job and position within the organization. If you want a promotion and want to advance, go to your supervisor; and then their boss. State your intentions, ask questions on the fastest way to do so; then, actually act in a manner in which they take you seriously. On the other hand, if you know you don't like your current job, embrace that; and better schedule your off-time to get into something you want to do. Be productive in your off-time to move in a direction you can see yourself in! See if you can setup meetings with people that do what you want to do; research, and then implement a plan to move in that manner.

- GET SOME LIFE INSURANCE and/or a pre-need burial plan (bought directly from a funeral home)! Do this for yourself and your parents if it has not already been done. I know it sounds kind of morbid and you probably don't want to think about things like this; but, it's a fact of life. This is very important in the black community because we tend not to think about this type of stuff until it's too late and we have to scrape up bill money, visit the pawn shop, start Go-Fund Me sites, and/or walk parking lots and intersections collecting donations to bury our loved ones. Save yourself the headache.

Please list any notes, questions, or concerns. (Search for exactly who you need to talk to in order to get your questions answered thoroughly, you might have to step out of your comfort zone and make some phone calls.):

_____

_____

_____

_____

_____

_____

_____

_____

Side note: If you have to pick up the
phone and make some phone
calls yourself, here are some
tips for phone etiquette:

Pose a greeting ("Hello… good
afternoon"), state your name and exactly
why you're calling. Then, get ready to
take down the name of the person you're
speaking with and the date. Be sure to
get their email/ direct number and send
them a thank you message after the
phone call. You might even want to
practice what you would like to say
before you make the call (make sure you
cover all the major points you need so
you want have to consistently call back).

Making Your Way Out:

Meaning—out the hood, out of your current circumstance, breaking that poverty cycle, being the first to go to a post-secondary educational institution. Basically winning "by any means necessary"—legally though!

If you're reading this book and you've gotten this far, then you are the one! You are the one to break all those dysfunctional chains in your life and in your family's lineage. You will be an exemplary example to your friends! And contrary to your beliefs, it starts with being just who you are and striving for a better life. If you see what you're surrounded by, you want a better life and you're willing to work for it; then, you're half way there!

Let me just start off by saying that doing something new is scary. I don't care who you are or what you're about to get into, be it positive or negative, doing something new is scary. Entering the real world, whether you have a plan or not, will be scary; and there's nothing wrong with admitting that. Within the black community, we are taught to suck a lot of emotional things up; be it fear, heartache or whatever. I've been in high school classrooms talking with seniors who try to act bad, bold, fearless, or indifferent about what's coming next. But in reality, they have no idea how they are going to deal with the real world within the next couple of months.

Maybe you're already out of school; or didn't finish, and the real world has already hit you hard and fast. If you're not able to talk openly about this; or, if you don't have a circle of friends that have some kind of perspective on your situation, it can make things feel like an even more hopeless situation. The first step is to decide to do something different or new. Change your circumstance. Remember, the definition of insanity is to do the same thing over and over; but, expect a different result. Change takes courage and faith because honestly, you don't know what will come out of your next efforts. The hardest part is getting over that fleeting emotion of fear and pushing through.

Now for many of you, the main thing that has been forced down your throat is "go to college." Traditional college has been preached as the Holy Grail basically to the point that most of us are brainwashed. Well, I'm here to tell you that's not the truth all the time. You have options when **you create options**. Many of you have talents that a traditional college can't necessarily nurture. For example, if you are a hands on person and you like to fix things and are very good at it; then, you probably need to go to a technical school.

If you go to a technical school that focuses on the kind of mechanics you are interested in, you can graduate in a year or so and go straight into that field of work. Network within that field; and attach yourself to a positive mentor. Learn the business while working for others; but at the same time, start saving money and take some business and bookkeeping classes on the side to further understand that profession. This will allow you to one day move out on your own and build your own business. Don't get me wrong, achieving this feat won't be a walk in the park; nor is it for the faint of heart and spirit. But, it can be done.

Conquering the Institution of College: The Start of a Journey

Honestly, the "institution" of college was the **start of finding my way out**. I was a good student. I knew how to play the game of school anyway; but I knew nothing else because I didn't really cultivate my other talents (due to lack of finances and a bit of self-doubt). I was pretty timid and hadn't been exposed too much as far as business ownership, how to create passive steams of income; or, how to capitalize upon my other talents. I'm just now tapping into; and gaining confidence in, myself and the business knowledge that I've been building for the last couple of years.

College should not be approached as the end all and be all solution as far as, "oh this is what will get me out of the hood or my current situation." The process of **starting and finishing** college should be looked at as one of the first steps in learning "how to learn." It's a time to build yourself. I know that probably sounds stupid, but think about it. The entire time you went through secondary school (middle and high school), were you really taught how to learn beyond the material being presented to you?

Speaking as a former public school student, you were probably taught to a state exam (not at your teachers' discretion; but to that of an unconcerned state board pushing book publishing agendas). There's no teaching outside of the box. In fact, they punish teachers who do so. The books are full of half-truths (if you were lucky enough to even get an up to date version), the classes offered (outside of the core curriculum) are very limited; and, don't include employable trades any more like carpentry, mechanics, or computer engineering.

Because of this, we—in the black community—are cultivating a class of students with no imagination; moving from grade to grade without developing a learning map within their own brains to allow them to conceptualize and solve problems outside the classroom. In many cases, an elevated type of thought process isn't tapped into until we get to higher levels of education (which a majority don't reach—not because of a lack of ability, but a lack of money and exposure to other possibilities).

As a graduating high school senior, I had taken all the steps to go straight into college (like taking SAT/ACT testing early, applying to scholarships, and applying to schools for early admission). I had help doing all of this, from teachers to counselors to church members. (If you show others that you are serious, they will take you seriously.) I enrolled in a college prep program called Upward Bound—an organization spread throughout the country that provides 1st generation college bound high school students with college-level classes and preparation needed to gain college admission.

So basically, what I'm trying to highlight is the fact that you don't have to do this all alone. You have assistance at your disposal; particularly your high school counselors. Even your prospective colleges' admission staff will help you, to a certain extent, depending on how well you continue to ask for help. Also, understand that you will need recommendation letters from people that you have made impressions on (hopefully good ones). If you request a letter from them, you have to be professional and courteous in respecting their time. If the letter is due in 4 weeks, don't wait and spring it on them a week out from the date. Time is money and you have to respect other's schedules. Once you commit to the process of applying to school (or any kind of project with a timeframe), don't slack on upholding a schedule, because life is all about discipline and adhering to deadlines.

What are some areas or majors of study you may be interested in?

1. _____

2. _____

3. _____

4. _____

5. _____

Task: Call an advisor from a college/program you are interested in. You may need to find out where (geographically) the programs of your interests are located. Ask questions pertaining to what kind of timeline you're looking at to complete that program (the number of semesters of school you may need and if that profession requires you to get a license after graduation). Find a professional in your desired field. What advice can they give you about school options? [Be as respectful as possible when doing this. But if someone is just a complete asshole to you while you're figuring this stuff out, don't charge it to that school or profession; just move along to the next person that can help you.]

NetFlix *A Different World*

(This throwback series highlighted the black college experience)

College, for me, was an overall great experience; and one in which I got to experience, for free, thanks to scholarships. I experienced the good, the bad, and the ugly when gaining a college education on a traditional private white college. I attended Texas Christian University (TCU); a majority white school, so this is my personal experience in that environment. (At the time I entered the school, the entire minority population was about 18% collectively—meaning Black, Hispanic, International, etc. were all included in that 18%.) I can't speak for anyone else's experience of a campus with a fairly mixed or all black population; or, for what someone may experience on a smaller community college campus.

The first two years of college are basics; kind of like high school on steroids. This is because there is no one to baby you by standing in the halls telling you to get to class like in high school. It's expected that you go to every class, complete every assignment without an instructor reminding you, get independent tutoring via a professor's office hours or free help-clinics on campus; and actually read thoroughly and study effectively. The last two years (depending on the program you enter) are more focused on your major and your interests. Concepts studied can range from very abstract to very distinctive. You are called on to actually think (I mean outside your everyday frame of mind).

Personally, I had to pull on everything I thought I knew **and** had to learn what some of those "privileged" white kids already understood via the experiences that their well-to-do parents had already exposed them to (family businesses, worldly travel experience, private industry lingo, their associations with certain elite clubs and leagues, etc.). In short, I had to catch up and be ready to play just as hard as they were already equipped to do so; **while trying to match their confidence**.

> **Personal Advice**: DO NOT for one second let the air of attending a "white college" or any college for that matter, scare you out of the confidence you should have before you enter that school! Truthfully, I experienced this first hand. I attended college at two predominately white private universities in Texas (SMU and TCU) where student-on-student racial discrimination was; and still is, known to occur. I physicked myself out the first couple of semesters. I thought those white kids would be so far ahead of me academically that I didn't think I could hang. Well, that's before I found out how average most of them were (and many below average). I had a harder work ethic than the majority of them. This type of work ethic, coupled with my willingness to visit professor's office hours when I needed help; and a willingness to actively participate in class made getting through classes with As and Bs easy. Know that no one is better than you; or more deserving than you just because they are white. You have to know that first!

You can gain more exposure to the other side of business and social operations by joining various clubs and leagues on campus that are focused on your interests (no matter what your major may be). Get involved, go on trips, and participate in meetings. This is a great networking opportunity that allows you to meet people and learn things you wouldn't have otherwise been exposed to.

College is truly a time of self-exploration; while at the same time maintaining some sense of responsibility. Don't go and straight wile-out—you might just blow a once in a lifetime opportunity; especially if you're on scholarship. Four years will fly by! During this time, you need to be focused on the end goal—graduation and acquiring the 3 essential keys coined by Professor James Small [intro to his work found in chapter 5], training, tooling, and acquiring skills.

There's an agenda: we aren't sending you to college to get a job anymore. Your generation now has a greater responsibility. The goal is no longer assimilation, but domination and ingenuity. Observe and learn the ways that business and other platforms operate. Spot deficiencies, innovate solutions, and bring that knowledge back to the black community. College doesn't have to be just some mundane set of classes you attend. You can master your experience.

Remember that your major doesn't necessarily pigeon-hole you into a particular field; so, enter a program that interests you so that you will remain engaged in classes. Please consider visiting your academic advisors **every semester while in college** to make sure you are on track to graduate on time. I offer this precaution because I worked at a college advisors office and saw countless seniors turn in graduation applications (yes, you have to turn in an application to graduate from college); only to sadly be informed that they had another 2 or 3 classes to complete for their degree plan. You don't want to be the one who has ordered graduation pics and invitations only to find out that **you ain't really graduating**☹. Even if they let you walk across the stage, it won't be the same; only because that next semester you will still be attending class.

Now after graduation, I continued straight through graduate school for a Masters. I can't even lie, I did it because I didn't want to start working yet. I also had some fellowship (scholarship) funds that wouldn't be there the next year had I started working right out of under grad. I remember sitting in a prep class for the GRE (a test you have to take to enter grad school similar to taking the SATs for college); and the guy explicitly stated that going to grad school because you don't want to work is a bad idea. Well, he was wrong! At least in my case.

Don't ever let someone else tell you what's best for your situation when they don't know your situation. I was one semester away from graduating from college, but I didn't feel completely ready to enter "the real world." Something was missing. I was able to attend and finish grad school with 100% scholarship because of the timing in which I went.

Grad school totally elevated my frame of self-learning— meaning, I finally begin to understand that true education hinges on personal discovery and research much more so than any classroom lecture or syllabus outline. I began to understand that lectures and structured readings can only enhance what I learn on my own. And furthermore, independent study helped me understand how and when to properly challenge what was being presented to me in a classroom; or, in a news article or on TV. You have to trust your own abilities to disseminate information and come up with a solution to an actual problem in theory and real life. The ability to do this is especially crucial in these times because of how quickly technology is advancing and the large amount of information being force fed via media outlets (mostly lies).

On a personal tip, the year and a half that I spent in graduate school—secluded from my family—allowed me to reach some personal epiphanies. I was so used to taking care of everybody else and being the main child in the house helping my mother tie up the loose end that I realized I didn't know how to take care of myself. I learned how to put my needs first. I couldn't worry about what bills my mama had at her house, whether my little brother and his wife had everything they needed for their two toddlers; or, whether my other little brother had money on his books in prison. My survival and my education were my focus.

This experience is why I say college is just the first step; as self-education should follow in order to cultivate a hustler's mentality and ensure one's ability to survive inside and outside of their comfort zone once you enter the real world. You may find that when you graduate from college (with this "all powerful degree") that you can't get a job. They will tell you that you have no "experience." That's when you have to get creative with that résumé; including all those clubs that you joined, along with all of the activities (on and off campus) that you helped coordinate. It's also the time when you're hustlin' mentality kicks in [see "Boss Status" for more details]. Did you pick up a side-hustle while in college? Did you go to the City Clerk's office and file a DBA in order to be a registered business owner? It's all in how you market yourself and your abilities!

The college experience:

- o **Preparation for school**: When buying supplies and stuff, don't overdo it. During the first semester, people end up buying a whole bunch of stuff they probably won't even use. When preparing for class and buying books, definitely buy used. You may be able to email your professor before class starts to get the book list early so that you can order them from other places than the campus bookstore; like, Amazon, eBay, or just google 'cheap textbooks' (hardcopy and digital). You might even consider buying the previous edition—which will be much cheaper—if there aren't too many changes.

- o **Class Act**: Not every class you take will be interesting, but that really doesn't matter. You have to participate in that class almost as if your life depended on it. 1) The instructor should know your name (no matter how many students are in the class). You should sit relatively close to the front of the class and ask questions; or, make valuable comments when appropriate. 2) Readings for class are the very core of the class, so you should read them ALL! They may be boring, but you're going to have to pull some mind-tricks! Just trick yourself into thinking it is the most interesting subject ever. You may actually have to read chapters aloud to yourself. (Just remember you're paying for these classes; so you might as well get some kind of information out of it for your personal use.) If you find yourself in a situation with a certain class, learn about your withdrawal options. Find out what effects it would have on your financial aid and your grades for the semester. Make the best decision for you and your situation.

o **Actually learn how to study:** This is very important: especially if you're going straight to college from high school without taking a couple of buffer summer college classes. You **cannot** get away with last minute "studying" like in high school. I made A's in high school and thought I had it down. No boo-boo, I was wrong. This is a totally different ball park. It's not hard, it's just different and requires much more effort and thought. Understand the syllabus and your own scheduling. Do you concentrate better at night or in the morning? When should you schedule times to meet with the professor if you find yourself struggling, etc.? Remove all distractions from your space. I actually had to put my TV in the closet my 1st semester. Take the time to understand how grading will be computed and which assignments are the major tests/papers/projects. Start those early so you will have time to run your progress over with the professor (nine times out of ten they will tell you exactly how they want something done if you hit them up early, guaranteeing an A or B).

o **Independence:** Scheduling is probably one of the most important aspects of surviving your 1st semester. You need to estimate a proper time to get from class to class, incorporate lunch, have enough time in between classes to finish assignments; and manage a work schedule. For a lot of y'all, this may be your first time completely away from home. You'll set the time and priority in which you do everything and if you find yourself in a bit of trouble; it will be on you. Leaving home may be a relief in a sense; especially if you had more responsibilities than most others. Balancing this independence will be tricky, but enjoy this **time to do you**. At the same time, you will have to step up your game and make sure you are on top of your business— handling pressures of class, work, and personal issues). There are no excuses not to because at this point, **you're grown!**

- o **Mixing it up (campus involvement)**: Depending on the type of university you attend (a HBCU, a public, private, or junior college), the environment will be very different from your high school. Because I attended a smaller private white university, I was blessed enough to have a close-knit "black hole" (the black community on campus). In whatever type of environment you find yourself in, know that this is the time you should consistently step out of your comfort zone. You should make it a priority to fully engage in your new environment. This can be done by interacting with others outside of your culture, developing a tolerance, and having to be the example of the black race for those that have little or no interaction with blacks (so they may have many stereotypical views). You should join campus clubs and help organize programs; as you'll eventually find your fit. Trust me, you will probably never have another time in your life as free as your college years! Don't let that experience slip away.

- o **Frats & Sororities**: This is one piece of college a lot of #YBAs are most excited about. The 1st thing about the subject to consider is the reasoning behind why you want to join a frat or sorority. You should write this down in order to have something to compare to the organization's purpose in which you want to join. Also, evaluate if their actions as an organization match what they actually claim is their purpose. I didn't join a sorority during my under grad years because of timing and the brunt of my personal responsibilities; but enough of my close friends pledged so I got some insight on the pledging process. I basically decided for myself that I was too grown for a lot of the pettiness that took place on my campus. However, as a whole, I have to say that I appreciate black frats and sororities for what they do. (Special thanks to the Metropolitan Dallas Alumnae Chapter who awarded me with one of my scholarships!)

College will be a whole new experience; full of balancing responsibilities, matched by the freedom to dodge those same responsibilities. You will have to pick up some discipline and learn to fend for yourself. For some of you, you may have been doing this for some time now. Some of you actually have been responsible for not only yourself; but, for your family at large (i.e. being a caregiver of a family member or paying household bills, etc.)!

I was a co-provider in my household—helping pay water, lights, rent, or whatever else we might have needed, at times. It was a struggle transitioning from high school to college mainly because I was consistently being pulled in two directions. On one hand, you start a new life as an independent student; while on the other hand, your family still has a pig-tie on you and your duties to the house (especially if you go to a local college).

It didn't matter if I had a major mid-term exam or a paper due, my mama still would call me in the middle of a study session to let me know how much she needed for a portion of the rent or when the termination notice for the light bill came. This can be extremely trying; to say the least! I had asked her several times before not to call me with stuff like that because I was already under the pressure of keeping up in class, maintaining my scholarships, and working "X" amount of hours at my part-time job (which was basically almost full-time). This plea didn't stop the calls from coming.

If you find yourself in this situation, you have to break this cycle; or, it will become detrimental to your ability to focus in school, as well as put a strain on your family relationships. They will still demand your time and money—things you don't really have the ability to part with without putting yourself at risk of failing. More importantly, you need to understand that **it's not being selfish** to tell your family NO! It's what you need to do in order to survive and better yourself.

This process, resulting in you finally saying "no" when requested to provide financial help or to sacrifice your time or emotions, is not an easy one. Honestly, backlash from the borrowing family member will likely follow. This may take the form of cutting you off, cursing you out, making you feel guilty, etc. Don't fall for it! It was meant to hurt your feelings; it was meant to make you feel so bad that you give into them and let them drain you again and again. You just have to pray and move on. I promise you they will come around at some point; probably around graduation time when they won't stop bragging on you, but; they'll neglect to tell the story about how they cursed you out months before. Been there done that; and have more than a handful of friends that experienced the very same thing.

You owe it to yourself to do what you need to do for yourself; and if family members can't or don't understand that, then, they're the ones being selfish!

Learning in Action
How many millionaires can you list that don't have a college degree? Your list probably consists solely of famous people. But, as I sat in my first entrepreneurial college class, my business professor stated that the average millionaire was more likely to own a business dealing in everyday necessities of life (i.e. plumbing, janitorial services, landscaping, etc.).

This shocked the shit out of me! In my head—at the time—if you had some paper on you and you weren't a famous entertainer (or an infamous drug dealer), then I assumed that you had to be some big shot Wall Street suit and tie guy that had an MBA from a top ranked school. Apparently, that's not always the case.

In most of the high school classrooms I've visited, one of the first questions I have asked is, "What are you going to do after you graduate?" Many times, I've posed this question to seniors during their last semester of school with graduation approaching within the next 6 weeks or so. I bet you can guess what the unanimous answer was. "I'm going to college." But their facial expression had that "I guess I am" look.

My next set of questions to each person would be, "Where did you apply? Have you received your acceptance letter?" Half of the kids would return a response like, "Well… I haven't applied yet." Thoughts in my own head: "What the hell! You graduate in 6 weeks, claim you're going to college and you haven't even applied to a school—not one (community college, a four year university, or a technical trade program)! You've got to be kidding me." But aloud, I respond, "Is that really what you want to do?"

I already knew that they really didn't want to go. I asked a couple of these "maybe babies" why they responded that they were going to college when it's clear that they aren't sure about it. No one could give me an answer. This was because the answer they originally gave was probably something their parents told them, probably an ultimatum: you either work or you go to school; or, you get out of my house. Have you; or an older sibling, ever been in this situation?

Let me say this, **"College ain't for everybody!"** (Don't use this as an excuse not to go if you're just scared; if you're capable and able THEN GO.) The realities of the real world are that everyone will not go to college. This is what we in the black community need to tell our black youth whom are very iffy about going to college; especially those that have been force fed the ideal and think it's their only option. Let me say it again because I know you probably think you read that wrong. **School ain't for everybody and you ain't got to go; especially if it's not your real desire**. Now that's something I know you don't hear on a regular, primarily because everyone is usually trying to brainwash you into thinking college is the only way you can make it.

With that being said, take heed to this cautionary note: 1) success is not guaranteed to most whether they are "degreed-up" or not; 2) doing anything without some level of experience (whether that be collegiate or through street knowledge and experience) is almost always detrimental.

Now here comes my disclaimer. As I explained in the previous section, I went to college in the traditional sense, 4 years at a university and 1 ½ years of graduate school. My experience was priceless. The friends I gained have been more reliable than most I acquired through high school; and, I have no doubt that the degrees I completed led the way for me to secure the government job that I have now. Because I moved through the motion as prescribed, I was able to earn a secure income, get a house by the age of 25, save a couple of pennies, go on a couple of nice vacations… live the "American Dream" at least for a little while until I woke up.

Consciousness began to knock on my door. I realized that if I didn't take control of my life and engage in following my own personal desires, I would remain stuck in "the matrix" and settle for working some job for the next 40 years. Once you get caught up in the system, you continue to perpetuate it by having to work (mostly for somebody else) to maintain things that you have acquired (a car, a house, and thousands in student loans). Well, when do you start living life?

Depending on what **you** want to do with your life, college in the traditional sense doesn't have to be the very thing that makes or breaks you. Again I reiterate, it depends on what **you** want to do. Going to college for your parents or because that's what society says you should do isn't necessarily the answer to your situation.

My underlying point is that school cannot and will not give you all of the answers. As #YBAs, you should step outside the box in your educational endeavors. Our kids should have coding classes, tax classes, technical and trade classes throughout middle school and high school; giving them a true chance to understand who they are and what they are actually good at. Especially those kids with "learning disorders" who have other talents that far exceed what they are doing in the classroom. Denying that kid that opportunity to exceed is cheating the world of their creativity because societal measures have crushed them and placed their ability in a box; while killing their confidence.

Experience, willpower, and a strong work ethic tend to separate the successful from the unsuccessful stories. These things could make all the difference in **your** story of success. Let your desire drive you and supplement a formal education with an alternative form (technical/trade school, an apprenticeship, an internship, in addition to **independent study**) to get up on game and position yourself where you want to be.

For example, say that you are about to graduate high school—with no intentions of going to college, but you know that you are very fascinated with cars. You may be lucky enough to have a mechanics class in your high school, which you should make every effort to enroll. If you want to further your knowledge on cars then you're right if you have no interests in attending a traditional college. Let's be honest, what in the hell will enrolling in a traditional college do besides waste your time and money?

Once you graduate from high school, you can work a part-time job (or take up a small loan) to pay for an **accredited** automotive technical school program that's only one and a half years long (versus spending 4 years in a major you have no interests in). To take full advantage of your training, the best thing you could do is build a solid reputation with instructors. Establish trust in your work and character. Pull knowledge and connections from instructors; a word or two from the people they know could open opportunities up to work at a dealership via an externship (during which you can gain real-work experience). This allows you to capitalize on that experience by understanding how the actual work is done; and, how the business is handled behind the scenes.

Now you have just given yourself options upon graduation of your program: 1) based on your work at the externship you could get hired immediately following graduation; 2) with the experience you have gained you can apply for better positions elsewhere; 3) now that you have experience in the field, you can further revaluate your goals for the future. You can begin to answer questions you probably had no idea about before. Do you want to move up in status as a supervisor or manager of repairs? Or, do you see yourself moving into ownership of your own garage at some point? Understand that if you choose to move into ownership or management that it may require you to supplement your experience with some classroom work via online; or, in-class hours or the completion of a career specific certificate. Crucial classes you may need include management and leadership classes; coupled with payroll or accounting basics.

Do you see how you can make that work if that's your passion? Now, how can you relate this example to your interests and passions? Imagine if your desire and interest was in technology as a program coder. These are the types of hobbies that lead to multi-million dollar start-ups (i.e. Facebook and SnapChat). Now, I did have one student in one of my classes straight up tell me that she wasn't going to college. I asked her what she planned on doing; and she actually had an answer. She told me that she had already found a welding program she was about to enter. Most of the other kids started laughing at her. This program would only be about a year and half long; and when she graduates from the program, the base pay for the skill of welding starts at about $50/hr (depending on locality). She further continued to say that if she decided to get involved in underwater welding, the pay base would start at $80/hr. She shut everybody in that room up! I was kind of impressed; and I congratulated her for having a plan in life.

Write down your **true** interests.

_____

_____

_____

_____

_____

Write down some possibilities/dreams about those interests.

_____

_____

_____

_____

_____

How could you get hands on experience in that particular field of interest?

_____

_____

_____

_____

_____

The hardest thing about forgoing college is the fact that it's a more involved and hands-on task that you're taking on. You will have to carve your own path. See, when you go to college, you get a counselor who hands you a prepared checklist with the classes you must complete based on you major. It may even include some suggested internships to look into your junior/senior year. On a nontraditional path, you don't have that luxury.

There's no safe haven of school and staff-provided counseling centers; and that can be scary. But by the same token, the rewards can be far greater than just getting a standard job like most college graduates. You will have a certain freedom in how you choose to accomplish your passions. However, because you have no safe haven or cookie-cutter plan at your disposal, you have to be ready to grind; and I really mean be ready to grind—working long hours, at times.

Certain things that you may be interested in may cost you money in order to obtain the training. Unlike traditional school, financial aid may not be available. This may mean picking up a couple of extra shifts; or, getting another part-time job besides the full-time job you may already have. While a college student would have the opportunity to just get a federal loan without putting in any work. Remember that you're on a different path. Just in case you still think your aspirations are out of reach, google the stories of these "kid-preneurs": Moziah Bridges, Jaden Wheeler & Amaya Selmon (brother and sister), Leanna Archer, and Maya Penn.

The Service Route

Another major option many #YBAs look into upon graduation from high school is entry into the service. Now in reference to those of you thinking about joining the armed forces as a young black person—especially straight out of high school, please be extremely careful. I want to make this very clear. Understand that when we as a country "go to war", it's basically a gleam in the eye of every major corporation in the US because going to war means going to the bank. It seems like the biggest concern is the amount of money to be spent. Supplies are needed in order to conduct a "war." From the crappy dried foods sent to soldiers in the field, to the boots they wear out, to the planes they fly and the boat repairs the Navy requests. Who do you think services those requests; and how much money do you think they make off of such services? Billions on top of billions of tax dollars (your $). A soldier's life seems to be but a commodity at times of war.

So, if you're going to do this, you have to do this right! First of all, a lot of us join the Army (or any other branch: Navy, Marines, Air Force, National Guard) to pay for school. Or, we join because we think the government will give you some kind of invaluable skill for your service. You have to learn to play the game like those at the top of the food chain. Know and understand the differences between entering in as a bottom-level enlistment versus an officer of a specific career field.

You **don't** have to enlist in the service right out of high school to get college paid for! This is one of the biggest misconceptions. You see, you can go to college (use federal loans—wisely), without enrolling in the service; or the campus ROTC on campus, have a fantastically stress-free four year experience, graduate and then enlist in service as an officer in your field (medicine, law, engineering, etc.) and get paid twice, or even 3x as much, as a high school enlistment. Depending on your career field, you can potentially choose where you want to be stationed. All of this, of course, is pending availability and budgets on the behalf of the government.

Understand that in times of duress, recruiters will lie to you! They have quotas to meet and they will easily trade 4-8years of your life in order to make their monthly enlistment quotas. So, you need to arm yourself with knowledge and questions that will benefit you. The armed services will also promise you retirement at 20 years of service. But what they don't tell you is, that they can and will off-set your retirement date if they decide to deploy you for who knows how long.

At the point of signing up for the armed services, you lose a certain level of autonomy over your life. It shocked me to find out that if you are under active duty as a female and give birth, they command you not to breastfeed your own child because they don't want the child to get too attached to you. After your six weeks of maternity leave is up, they can then deploy you, SMH. You don't even have the choice of how you want to feed you own child. What kind of shit is that?

My point is that you need to understand **all** of the benefits and limitations upfront—work the system, don't let it work you. See, you have high-level politicians working this system to a much higher degree with their children. That's why they ain't afraid to go to "war" because they know that their sons and daughters won't be on the battlefield; but behind a desk while Jerrika, Terrance, and Jose (breadwinners of their family) lose a limb or die on the front lines. That's real.

The Real Scoop on Teen SEX:

Sound Track: J. Cole "Wet Dreams"

As much pressure as it is out here to have sex, there doesn't seem to be enough education on the after effects of having **immature sex without intimacy**. That is, until you are dealing with a result of it by way of teen pregnancy, STD/STI transmittal, and/or the realization that your partner may be sleeping with several other people. All things aside from the moral and religious stigma associated with teenage sexual activity, let's first talk about what I mean by "immature sex without intimacy." I'm talking about the large number of kids having sexual encounters at ages where they couldn't possibly understand the physical and emotional baggage that comes along with the after effects of sex.

Today, sex is bought and sold; then posted for display. For example, everybody and they mama got a sex tape and can sell them for millions (i.e. Kim K, MIMI from LHHA, and Rick Ross (the rapper) baby mama). This is done so often that all the emotion that goes into sex is overshadowed. As a pre-teen/teen consumer, you're sold a lie that depicts sex as a meaningless action. The truth is that it can be the most devastating issue you deal with if you're not ready to deal with all of the responsibility and vulnerability immature sex exposes you to.

Then, on top of that, you have to be extra careful not to get caught in a sex-scandal; taking into consideration the use of cell phones, photos, videos and social media. Pics and videos are easily leaked. This can result in your naked selfie—sent to your partner in confidence—going viral across your school, or worse. (I mean it could happen to you.) Not to mention the fact that sexting is a felony now in some states; even if you're under age—so you could get in serious trouble just for sending the picture.

Case in point, a 17 year old black athlete (football, basketball, and wrestler) at Parkway High, by the name of Levar Allen of Louisiana got arrested and charged with contributing to the delinquency of a juvenile and possession of child pornography. [Please Google the entire story] Why? Because a 16 year old **white** girl (his classmate) sent him a nude video **first**; which he then sent her a video, in response. The girl's parents found out about it and called the police on him! Now, this brother is facing 10 years in jail. (My home-girl calls it the new millennium Emmet Till case.)

To all my #YBBs (young black boys), when will y'all learn to leave "Becky with the good hair" alone? In the end, you will always be black—the predator—and they will always be white—the victim. It's called entrapment. [Please Google the story of Jack Johnson; and what his love for white women resulted in.]

Sex may seem very important right now, but if you engage in immature sex, especially without true intimacy (defined as knowing, trusting, and loving yourself, **then** knowing, trusting, and loving a **committed** partner), it will hurt you in the long run. Make sure you're both on the same page. Don't assume anything! If the both of you haven't had a discussion where you have drawn definitive lines of a committed relationship, then you ain't in one—PERIOD.

If he/she has not said "we are boyfriend/girlfriend/fiancé and that these are the rules of our relationship, then don't be surprised if you sleep with them on that assumption and they're sleeping with several other people, as well. Remember, to "assume" something is to make an ass out of "u" and "me." (Hell, you still have to be a little suspicious if titles, rules, and boundaries have been set—people lie.) Getting into this type of predicament will propel you into a space of adulthood that you may not be ready for; a space that will surely rob you of your young adulthood full of carefree fun and dating without strings attached.

You have to understand how important emotional intelligence is within a relationship; yours and that of any potential partner. Sometimes someone can appear to have it all; but they fail to understand your feelings and how to make you feel secure and/or to be there for you emotionally. One of the best ways to see this is to see how your partner deals with a tragedy. Watch their actions. How do they protect your feelings in troubled times? Will they have your back; or, leave you high and dry when you really need them? Will they keep your confidence; or, go run and tell "everybody and they mama all yo business?"

One reason I remained abstinent so long (throughout high school, college, and grad school) is because I learned and understood things through the observation of others. I try not to make the same mistakes others have made; especially when I see them first hand. On my first day of high school, I saw 4 pregnant girls; and this was in just one lunch period!

I mean, they were full-fledged preggo—no maternity clothes, just belly hanging out over their jeans; with the top button undone. In my mind, I thought, "Oh hell no, won't be me!" I promised myself that I wouldn't have sex; at least until I graduated. I didn't want to be a statistic. On top of that, I would hear females and dudes both talking about where they "hit it" and I refused for my first time to be in a car, the field behind the school, a vacant apartment; or, in any of the crazy places I had heard. I had it in my mind that anybody I would be with would at last have his own apartment—with some decent furniture, at that!

I just thought it wasn't worth it. I saw these baby's daddies break up with their baby's mamas time and time again. I saw girls—shaped like coke bottles (Beyonce)—get on birth control (Depo-Provera was the most popular back then) just to sleep with these little boys. They thought they were avoiding the consequence of pregnancy. But, they ended up blowing the crap up because of the Depo shots. I mean FAT!

You have to recognize that there will always be a reaction to any decision you make (whether positive or negative). Because of all of this, I just decided not to play the "sex game" at all. This day and age, the notion of being in a committed relationship is few and far between; especially when you have to worry about whether your partner is having sex with a friend in school or even a teacher. SMH, sad; but very true.

For years, I had heard teachers tell me and other girls that the boys in school would mature at the next level. In elementary and middle school, teachers talked about boys being more focused in high school. Once I got to high school, I found out that that was a lie. Worse yet, when I got to college the dudes I ran into were talking the same damn game from high school— which my mama had already versed me on. In middle school, high school, and college, sex was a game for a lot of people (boys and girls, alike). I had just decided not to play! I decided to be an outsider and just watch.

I had one teacher in elementary who kept it all the way real. One of her former 6th grade students had come to visit our class. It was a girl who was then in the 8th grade. My teacher introduced her to the entire class; and the girl then started to tell us a little bit about how junior high would be (class schedules, the work, the teachers, etc.). She had this other little girl with her (around 1 year old or so). She kept calling the little girl her sister. After the 8th grade girl talked to us awhile, she left.

Immediately, my teacher dismissed the boys to go outside and play. I was a little pissed because she had never split us up like that and the boys were going to get extra time outside. Well, she closed the door after the last boy left and continued to give us girls "the business." She explained how that girl that had just left the room had that baby in 7th grade; and that it wasn't her little sister! She didn't go into any particular detail; but, she made sure to let us know that it was very easy to get yourself into some real trouble if you didn't watch yourself and you got caught up with these "little nasty boys"—as she put it. At 10 years old, it kind of blew my mind that this 8th grader had a little baby. All I was worried about before this was basketball and soft ball.

I would later have yet another reminder that sex wasn't anything I needed any time soon. You see, as I was in my second semester of 7th grade, I remember this girl going missing. She unenrolled from the school without any of us students seeing her. She hadn't been in class for like two weeks before one of the other students asked our English teacher what happened to her. I distinctly remember the teacher responding, "Trust me, you don't wanna know." I thought, "What tha heck does that mean?"

That next year she returned back to school. Everybody was quick to ask her where she had been. When she responded that she had a baby, I could've fell on the floor. Nobody believed her, at all! This was partially because we all thought she was gay—which she later came out during high school. She literally had to show us pictures of her in the hospital in the bed with the baby.

I realized that sex brought about more consequences than I was ready for. Freshmen year in college yielded a couple of female associates of mine dropping out due to pregnancies; only a few of which returned to finish. Freshmen year also yielded exposure to STDs/STIs (sexual transmitted diseases and infections). I would hear stories of guys (but mostly of girls) who ended up with STDs; and trust me, the word spreads quickly, especially on a college campus.

I remember one girl who will forever remain known as "herpes girl" on my undergrad campus. She got this nickname within the first eight or nine months of school. She gained initial notoriety on campus by winning one of the black fraternity's pageants as a freshman. So after that, all the dudes were after her. My assumption is that she got friendly with a few of them; or maybe just one—I don't know. Now I don't know if she already had it; or, if one of those dudes gave it to her, but, by the end of that school year she was known as "herpes girl," which is absolutely horrible. I mean, every time the girl came out of the campus nurse's building, someone would make a joke that she just got her herpes medicine.

Which brings me to my next point. Protect yourself! Get tested and suggest that your soon-to-be partner gets tested, too. If you're nervous about suggesting it, do it in a casual sort of manner like its normal to you; then they won't feel as offended. Be like, "Cool… it's been a minute since my last testing, we can just go together that way we can get our results at the same time." And now you can go buy AIDS tests in the store, and some testing centers offer free screenings. They even have "smart condoms" out there that will tell you if someone is HIV/AIDS positive. [Please Google to find more info.] The BET series *Being Mary Jane* has an epic scene where her partner comes over thinking he's about to get some and Mary Jane serves him up a platter full of at-home testing kits.

It's also important to remember that sex involves emotion; **as it's not just some random act**. In relationships, it is very important to pay attention to the way your partner handles your emotions. Early on in a relationship, pay attention to patterns of potential mates. Actually write down big behaviors or incidents that don't sit right with you. Look at how these behaviors and incidents progress over a time span of 3 months, 6 months, and 1 year. Are these incidents getting bigger? Are they escalating while negative patterns are beginning to cycle? That's a red flag.

YouTube "5 Keys to Identifying Your SoulMate"

(I normally don't pay attention to "cliché" messages with these type of titles, BUT this one is sooooooo on point. It is worth the 50 min listen. Please make time to view this message!)

The most important thing in this rollercoaster of your young relationships is to understand yourself and how you need to be loved. Fully evaluate if the person you're sharing such an intimate thing with is actually loving you, controlling you, and/or using you. It's hard enough to figure out exactly how you yourself need to be loved. So imagine how hard it is for two people to try to figure that out at the same time; with each other. My main point in saying that is, sometimes you may need to be alone and workout your own personal issues before jumping into relationships; especially sexually active relationships.

Now in the real world—outside of college—it gets even more complicated. You may encounter married individuals who may or may not tell you the truth about their situation. Having uneducated and immature sex with these individuals can and could lead to adultery, lies, disease, and embarrassment.

Upon your exit out of high school, you basically check your childhood at the door. More specifically, the arena of love, sex, and relationships becomes real. Some of y'all may have been doing the most in high school any way (having several partners, getting experienced in every type of position, or even messing around with adults already). (You may have even caught an STI, got a shot, been cured, and kept it moving.)You may think that there isn't much that you haven't already done and that it's only going to get better when you get out in the real world.

Let me tell you, getting involved in adult "sex-capades" can turn into a Jerry Springer circus if you're not careful. It's hard to step out of a situation with a married person when their spouse, kids, side-chicks/dudes are involved. My point is that you don't have to subject yourself to being caught up. Research, research, research! The least you can do is to know the person you're getting involved with on paper. It's not too hard to look up someone's criminal, job, and marital background via county records and online background checks.

Shoot, I know some of ya"ll be Facebook, Intsagram, & Twittter stalking anyway! Don't half ass the job, dive deep because if they ain't got nothing to hide; then, you should know what they have going on. It's real out here; did you know that in some states it's legal for trans-genders/sexuals to change their sex on their birth certificate; and all their state IDs [Google NCTE transequality.org/documents]? So, that means you probably need to see baby pictures and shit! Talk to a couple of their drunk aunts and uncles until one of those embarrassing stories surfaces. Families will hide their secrets for them; so you need to listen and watch everything.

In the same mouthful, on the subject of baby pictures, I offer this simple advice without judgment: don't rack up a team of baby-mamas or baby-daddies. Having kids early is hard enough; but having functional relationships with an attachment of multiple people is hard and can become really messy (look at Future and Ciara, Peter Gunz and Taira, etc.). Besides that, having kids too early will put a strain on your journey in finding yourself, your purpose, and what you ultimately want to do. It will then be your responsibility to watch over and provide for that child; your life and plans are then put on the backburner.

My main point is that you can't go back, once you're a parent (ANOTHER LIFE WILL THEN DEPEND ON YOU). The bad decisions you make don't just hurt you, they will hurt your kids. You have to set yourself up in a better situation to better incubate our next black generation; it's crucial!

For example, in one of the classrooms I spoke in, a student informed me of how her cousin had just graduated and can't get a job. We segued into this story when I started talking about the importance of maintaining your credit score and how to check your annual report [see "Ca$h & Your Ratchet Priorities"]. I was prefacing the importance of making sure no one uses your name and credit improperly. At this time, the student told this story and clarified that her cousin couldn't get a job because the cousin's mother had a drug problem, was in and out of jail; and, had used her daughter's name and birthday when they booked her. So now, that student's cousin has a criminal record because of the bad habits and decisions of the mother.

That was absolutely ridiculous. No parent should put their child in a situation like that. To have the strength to then go against your mother and file the proper charges against her for stealing your identity takes strength; and puts an additional emotional drain on you. Occurrences like these make the cycle of complete dysfunction continue to sink the black community; setting #YBAs back further behind the start line.

Just to clarify, I'm not condemning having kids, I'm just drawing the point that one should be stable enough to support kids—meaning being out of "yo mama house" and paying bills on your own, comfortably; and being in a good space with your partner. Think about some of the necessary things you didn't have (both parents in the house, a stable place to lay your head, a safe neighborhood, etc.). Would you like to see your kids have those things and better? Well, having babies early and getting on government assistance won't provide all those things you know that your future children deserve.

To those of you out there who still may approach sex irresponsibly; thinking that you can do whatever you want and fix the problem after the fact (I'm talking about abortion), I want to reiterate that all actions have a consequence. It's important to take care of yourself if you are sexually active. This is especially true if you don't want an unplanned pregnancy. The quick fix of an abortion isn't always the easy or the right answer. And for the guys, this isn't just a female issue.

I know a couple of girls that had abortions in high school. They grew up, got married, and now they can't have children with their husbands because of what they put their bodies through during high school and college. THAT'S A BIG CONSEQUENCE! Remember that there is no step-by-step instruction manual to life. Some things you set in motion may not be God's plan.

Ca$h & Your Ratchet Priorities

YouTube "The Truth about Money, Debt, & Taxes What They Don't Want you to Know"

Money is a big issue. Either you got it or you don't. Majority of us in the black community have disproportionately experienced the "don't" more than we would like. We can easily point at the fact that the system whipped us behind the curve from jump. American enterprises that still function today were no doubt built off of free black slave-labor.

We are dealing with a system that never respected us in the first place. Have you ever seen a wanted poster for a runaway slave before? The bounty on that slave's head most likely said "dead or alive." Now let's think for a minute here. Wouldn't a slave be worth more if brought back alive versus dead? The truth of the matter is that to the slave owner, it didn't matter much because that slave was probably insured by a bank (pretty much any conglomerate that still exists today). So if brought back dead, the slave owner could still collect a cash amount from the bank and go purchase another slave. How real is that?

Our financial situation as black people is at the core of our dysfunction and inability to compete with those of higher economic and social classes. The sad part is that our parents (at no complete fault of their own) inherently passed down the broken system of finance which increased our chances of failure.

At the heart of this, we have to understand that it is not our parents' fault. They are handing down the same situation upon which their parents had to survive on; and their parents before them, and so on and so forth until you get back to those share-cropping and slavery days where our ancestral line worked hard only to get slighted in the end. Well, those days are well over (figuratively speaking anyway); and that means it's time to switch the game up.

I'm going to tell the truth; as a #YBA myself, I didn't understand how to do this. I was scared of money. I didn't know how to use money as a tool versus just to pay bills. I know that 90% of you reading this are scared of money, too.

Your probably like, "What, I ain't scared of money! Shoot, if I had some money, I already know everything I would buy. I want money. I need money. I ain't scared of it."

Well let me tell you, you are scared of money. You're scared of being broke! Am I right? We are more afraid to spend money to make money than we are to just spend money frivolously to buy "stuff" that won't last; and will be out of style next year, SMH. As the next generation, it's your responsibility to learn **how** to use money and how to equip yourself well enough to play the money game "legally"; better than "they" have since the birth of this nation.

I came from a single-parent home, with one stream of income. By the time I got ready to go to college, the FASFA (Free Application for Federal Student Aid) people requested confirming information from me for 3 of the 4 years I applied for aid because my household income was like under $15,000 in a household of 4 people. In saying that, I was called on to become like the second parent in the household. I paid bills!

It was nothing to hand over a couple hundred dollars (made from braiding hair on the side) to keep the lights from getting cut off; or, my brothers helping my mother put gas in the car with money that they made mowing lawns or hustling snack cakes and candy bought with food stamps. The ghetto budget of "robbing Peter to pay Paul" almost kilt my mother; as it was a reality on those days that she cried because she couldn't do any better at the time. That was enough for me to say, "I won't be going through this again."

Because I was introduced to the necessity of money for pure survival (water, food, shelter, lights, etc.) I never really understood how to use money in the manner that it's supposed to be used, as a tool! Money isn't just used for survival. You should use money to make more money to better your life—the life you dream of—and thrive.

Financial responsibility

Sound Track: Save that money by Lil Dicky ft. Fetty Wap

For all of you out there supporting your household—through a part time job; or, a part-time hustle (legal or other)—there will come a time when your own survival will have to trump that of all the other people you are struggling to take care of. The prime lesson I've learned is, you can't help others if you can't help yourself; if you're not pouring into yourself, but serving everybody else, you're going to run your own well dry.

Financially, if you can't flex a one-handed push-up yourself, it doesn't make sense to body-build for others—meaning, at no point during your development into a financially secure adulthood should you be putting your own wellbeing in danger.

Now I'm not telling you to abandon a sick and/or elderly parent/guardian; or, someone dear to you who physically can't take care of themselves. I'm saying that your well-being cannot be sustained unless you build yourself. You can't hold others if your base is weak; or under-developed. I can preach this from experience. I was in that situation and if I don't stay focused I still find myself teetering back and forth between sacrificing my financial stability to help others that don't reciprocate. It's forever a constant battle.

When the lights get turned off at the house, it gets real. That $100 you were saving to get your first lap-top or whatever, seems less important, as you feel guilty for even having it. A hot shower for everyone in the house becomes more relevant.

I went off to college with pretty much a full ride; room and board with all bills paid, and, a cash car (bought with scholarship $). My only pressure should have been not to fail. But I was still carrying the weight of my four-family member household. That car I bought didn't sit in the student parking lot; it was at my mama house—frequently running up mileage when she went looking for my run-away little brother. It didn't matter that all my bills were covered at school because my mama sure would call me and remind me of what was due or about to be cut off at the house; all while I'm trying to read the 2nd or 3rd chapter assignment for the next day or finish a term paper due in the next couple of hours.

I had a job every year, sometimes two, working a couple of hours short of full-time; and spending money at home paying bills instead of saving up for my exit from college. I'mma paint a real picture: I came into college with probably over $120,000 in scholarships and left with about **-$40,000** in debt (I acquired by helping out at home). This was debt that I didn't necessarily need to get myself into. Now that doesn't make any sense, does it?

Don't do what I did and take on the burden of responsibilities of family (especially those that are out of your control); as it will bite you in the ass later on. You're still a child and should be working toward your own development. Don't feel guilty about doing just that! My junior year in college, I got myself in the greatest financial hole that I hope to never dig again. I risked my own credit and financial health for my mama, and the household in general, in a counterproductive way. I did this in the form of taking out student loans, paying bills that I should have never undertaken, and by trying to make other people comfortable (i.e. paying somebody else's bills). You have a responsibility to yourself to be more conscious and wise.

YouTube "How to get out of Debt on a low income"

(Please note that I do not endorse the highlighted website advertised at the end of the video, just the educational information discussed)

Let me be loud and clear in stating that you should not "loan" anybody any sum of money that you can't live without. If you cannot give them that money and forget about it; then, don't do it, especially via a credit card or any other form of credit (loan) because they just created a bill for you! I don't care if it's your mama, daddy, sister, brother, boyfriend/girlfriend you think you will one day marry, or a fiancé, for that matter. I use this as a rule of thumb from personal experience. 9 times out of 10 you will get screwed over!

You will live a portion of your life trying to pay off somebody else's debt while they won't even be worried about it (mainly because they are thinking about paying off a bill they have in their own name). Don't be a fool; no matter how much intention you think the person has to pay you back, action and intention are the difference between reality and monopoly money. This goes out especially to my females. You wouldn't imagine how many of my friends, including myself, would talk about being in a trusted relationship and being asked for money when your partner gets themselves in a jam... **Don't do it!**

My entire point behind saying this is to let that student who is; or maybe in the situation I was in, know not to make the same mistake I made. I set myself behind for others; then later learned my most expensive lesson. Most of the time when you give up or put up so much of yourself for others (even family members), they end up not fully appreciating it and/or they keep expecting you to do it over and over again to the detriment of yourself. Once you're depleted—used-up—those same people either won't or can't help you the way you need them to.

Point blank: don't take care of grown people when you can't take care of yourself to the standard for which you aspire to sustain. Never buy anything for somebody else in your name (that means co-sign too)! If they can't get it on their own, then they're not supposed to have it right now and that's not your fault or problem! This goes for your mama, daddy, sister, brother, boy/girlfriend, etc.

Now hopefully, for some of you this is not even an issue; and if it isn't, you should praise God right now. For some of you, the only issue you have to worry about is maintaining yourself and gaining your own financial stability after leaving your parent's house. The first step in this process will be to check your personal credit history.

Read *Rich Dad's Advisors: The ABC's of Getting out of Debt* budgeting audio cd and/or book

(May be in your local library)

You should check your credit report to ensure that no one (primarily a family member) put anything in your name and defaulted on it. To do this, you will need your social security number. If you have to mail in information to prove your identity, you may need a state ID as proof as to who you are. The primary free site where you can check your report is **www.annualcreditreport.com.**

Now, you have probably heard people mention their credit score. This site will not show you your credit score for fee, but you can purchase the option to see that information. If you already have a credit card in your name, some financial credit institutions have started to offer a **free** feature that will show you your credit score monthly.

It is very important to understand the basic nature of your credit report versus your credit score. First off, you don't have to pay anything to review your credit report. You can receive three free reports once a year. It's best to order them in intervals (for example, order one from a different credit agency during the time frame of January-April, then again May-August, then again September-December).

There are 3 national credit bureaus: TransUnion, Equifax, and Experian. They collect data from financial institutions that lend you money via car loans, home loans, credit cards/lines, etc. Your credit report consists of your social security number, address, employer, and all your credit/loan accounts in your name, collection accounts (if you have failed to pay back an institution for services—"defaulting on a loan"), and public records like bankruptcies, liens, and judgments against you. Other things you can find on your report are inquiries detailing what company has checked your credit (for example: if you apply for home utilities or a contract phone). Under each credit account, your report will list every month that you were to have paid and whether your payment was late or on time. An on time payment shows up green. A late payment will be yellow or red depending on how late it was; you never want a payment later than the month it was due in).

Google article titled "Seven secrets not on Credit Reports" from Fox Business to see what <u>does not</u> show up on your credit report

---

Now your credit score is like your report card for everything on your credit report as a whole. Banks and lenders use this number to gauge how risky it is to lend you money or to extend credit. This score can range from 300-850 with 300 being dangerously risky (basically you have no pull at the bank) and 850 being secure and stable (the bank will be knocking down your door trying to lend you money). Now if you are in high school or a couple of years out of high school you will probably not even have credit, as you have to build it strategically [see bullet points denoted with $$$ in "Graduation Fast Approaching"]. Your score will also determine the kind of rates (interest) the banks will charge you to pay off the loan you are asking for.

The higher your credit score, the least amount of interest the bank will charge you to borrow money. For example, if you and another person both take out a loan for $1,000 (by the way I'm talking about a legitimate loan from a bank or credit union, **not a PayDay Loan**—that's like signing up for slavery). Say you have a credit score of 750 and they have a lower score of 620, the bank may tell you that your interest rate on the loan will be 4.5% while the second person finds that the same bank offered them an interest rate of 7.5% for the same $1,000. Basically, you will end up paying ($1,000x 0.045) or $45 for borrowing the money (not including other fees charged) while the other person ends up paying ($1,000x 0.075) or $75 for borrowing the same amount of money; all because their credit score is lower.

Now that probably doesn't seem like such a big deal, right? I mean it's just $30 more. But, let's say you both go into a bank to get a loan for a house. You both ask for a $100k loan. Now, you're looking at paying ($100,000x 0.045) or $4,500 per year worth of interest for the term of the loan (usually 15 to 30 years until you pay off the principle balance of the loan) and the other individual is looking at ($100,000x 0.075) or $7,500 per year in interests. Notice, I said this is just the amount of interest per year; as it doesn't include your regular principle payment. I won't get too deep into this, I just want you to have a basic understanding. In order to further understand these terms thoroughly, please read Robert Kiyosaki's *Rich Dad Poor Dad for Teens*. You can probably find it in your public library.

Needless to say, your credit score is very important. It could save you hundreds of thousands of dollars during your lifetime if you understand how to maintain it. Checking your credit report regularly can help you keep tabs on accounts that have been opened in your name. It can also let you see whether they have been paid on time—this helps maintain a good credit score. Make sure you read up on financial wellness through books *like Finances for Dumbies* and Tamsen Bulter's *The*

Complete Guide to Personal Finance. Do this, especially before you graduate from high school before credit card companies start to target you and screw you over. If this has already happened, don't freak; as all the references in this chapter should give you plenty of options on how to clear up your credit.

It happens to the best of us. My mama, who has never used my or my brothers' credit—she gave us the chance to build or sink our own ship—told me that when I was like 3 months old, my granny put a South Western Bell phone in my name. (South Western Bell was like ATT in the 80s.) When my mother found out, she called the phone company and demanded that the phone be disconnected. When they disconnected the phone, my Granny proceeded to call and cursed my mama out for getting her phone turned off. Now how dysfunctional is that? SMH. It's like family members feel that they have a right to screw you over (in some cases before you can even talk).

You may want to talk to a financial advisor early on to lay some kind of positive financial direction. Seriously, look into doing this upon college graduation or upon getting your 1st full-time job. You also need to truly understand what it means to sign a contract (this includes phone contracts, leases, car/home, business or any other loan. [Google the five requirements of a valid contract.]

The Importance of getting an introduction to taxes:

After high school, the realities of the real world come quickly. One of those definite realities are taxes; and yes, you have to pay them. Federal (and state—depending on your location) taxes will be a constant subject for the rest of your life. There's an old saying, "the only thing certain is death and taxes." So you might as well do yourself a favor and get familiar with the 1040 Form and learn **how to file your own taxes**. This may sound overwhelming and quite frankly unnecessary, I mean H&R Block is right around the corner, right? The reason I say you should learn how to file your own taxes is because in the long run it could save you upwards of hundreds of thousands of dollars within your lifetime.

I'm not just referring to the amount of money you would pay a big tax preparer every year. Those hundreds of thousands of dollars also refer to tax breaks and deductions you could be taking advantage of as soon as you turn 18! The biggest tax deductions to utilize are those that pertain to small and home-based businesses. It's worth understanding how to write-off expenses like gas for your car, cell phone and internet usage; and even home utilities used in a home office space. The most relevant thing to know at this point may be understanding how taxes will affect you once you enter college; or get your first job while still living at home.

For example, if you are a college student, you can work, collect a check, still let your parents claim you as a dependent, and file taxes every year to get the money that the federal government took out of each of your checks. This will not necessarily affect your parents earned income credit unless you make over a certain amount of money for the year.

Did you know that every time your parents receive an income tax check, it means (depending on certain circumstances) that they over paid the government? What do I mean by over paying the government? Every pay check that you receive (unless you are a contracted worker) you have federal (and sometimes state taxes) taken out of your check. This amount is determined by the W-4 form you fill out once your employer hires you and gets your direct deposit information for your check.

Depending on the amount of exemptions you choose on your W-4 and the many legal deductions you can take throughout the year, the government will withhold a certain amount of your paycheck. Each exemption basically denotes the amount of people you take care of throughout the year. So if you get your first job and they hand you a W-4 form and you live with your parents or you live alone, you should probably just put 1 exemption. Now this decision depends on who's claiming to be head of household and whether or not you will simply files as a single individual (only responsible for yourself).

If at the time of your tax preparation you learn that you are getting a refund (again depending on certain circumstances); then, that means that the government got to keep money that was withheld from your paycheck for the greater part of the year without paying you interests on said money. On top of that, if you choose to go to H&R Block or Liberty Tax or any other major/minor tax chain, then that vendor will charge you a service fee anywhere from $100 to $400+ depending on how many supplemental forms they filled out for you.

FYI, you may need to be a little leery of smaller tax chains because at any point in time (especially if it's one of those here today gone tomorrow tax shops), they could compromise your personal info, which could easily lead to identity theft. Another thing, if a fly-by-night tax service executed the filing of your taxes incorrectly and they don't fully understand taxes, they probably won't offer you any protection if the federal government comes after you.

So I'm saying all of this to say, what better way to protect yourself than to take one or two tax classes to at least be familiar with what's going on. You should be able to read your tax report from a preparer, if not file them completely on your own. You can take tax classes at your local community college; or, you could go to one of those major chains, pay to take their tax-preparer class, and work a tax season with them. By doing this, you learn how things really work. If you decide you want to start doing taxes independently, you can write the money you spent taking the classes in the first place. You just started your side hustle for fee!

GUNS AND BUTTER

YouTube "Why black kids inherit dust"

(Pay special attention @ mark 4:20)

In the movie *Baby Boy,* Ving Rhames character Melvin went on to tell Lil Jody (Tyrese Gibson) the difference between guns-and-butter; and the art of bartering. Believe it or not, that's a real discussion that needs to be had in the black community. What Melvin was trying to explain to Jody is that flossing doesn't always equate to having money (a substantial financial concept). I ask you this, how many times have you heard the rags-to-riches... back to rags story?

Negros hit it big, gain a little fame and money, then lose it all within a couple of years because of bad money habits and/or tax debt! A lot of it is just financial ignorance. Real life examples: Terrell Owens, Wesley Snipes, Trinidad James, MC Hammer (the poster-child), and the list goes on and on. Every situation is different; but for the most part, lavish living well beyond their means put these celebrities in positions where they were in more debt than they could handle. When you look at how celebs spend their money, the average person almost flips at some of the "unnecessary" luxuries they buy. But truthfully, "us regular" people do the same stupid shit; just on a smaller scale. I promise you there's a homeless person that would be looking at a rather pricy purchase that you or your parents have made like, "Man that is crazy, I wouldn't have wasted money like that."

So let's look at the smaller scale. Say that upon graduation from college (if you choose the traditional route), you are lucky enough to land a decent job. At this point, you can start building up your guns. You probably will be looking to move out of your parents' house into an apartment; and buy a newer car (probably financing about $20k). After getting settled and earning a steady income, you will probably look for a more accommodating apartment or house (pricing greatly depends on your location and region). Let's say a decent place in Texas is around $100-160K mortgage.

> **Quick Tip:** When renting your 1st apartment, a lot more goes into it than coming up with the deposit and picking your desired cable package (butter, you really don't need). Apartment complexes review your credit, rental history, and your income ($ from a job or self-run business). If you don't have rental history (previous lease agreements that you have successfully fulfilled), then it is very likely that they will require you to obtain a co-signer.
>
> This will probably suck the most because you have to find somebody that hasn't jacked their credit up and that makes enough $ on paper to cover your rent in the event that you fail to pay. With rental history, apartment complexes also search to see if you have any previous broken leases (where you failed to pay out your lease agreement and moved out early or got evicted). Trust me these are bad.
>
> One of my brothers has several of these and because of this, none of the decent apartments around will rent to him. There were a couple of times he had to put my mama down as a "reference" saying he stayed with her so she could pose as the landlord when a prospective apartment complex considered leasing to him.
>
> Another option you may consider is to rent a house from a single landlord vs. a corporate owned complex. They usually go a little easier on the credit and background checks (yes they check to see if you have felonies) and are more

willing to give you a first, second, and third chance.

Once you get comfortable, and make a promotion or two, you will start thinking about spending money on butter (defined as anything extra—usually things you buy to impress others).

Honestly, a lot of us never even get to this point because we're caught up on butter and stuntin' on others before even establishing our guns (i.e. a reliable car, an affordable living situation, building a comfortable emergency savings account). Here's an example, you live with your parent(s); instead of saving for your own place or acquiring some kind of asset that could later yield you a profit (a home-based business or some real estate), you buy rims for your car—that's DUMB! The 2gs you just spent or worse yet, financed at Rent-A-Tire in no way makes your car run any better. You also increase the risk of blowing out a tire; which will ultimately cost more for you to get the flat fixed. But backwards people do it all the time—frontin' on the Vine and Intsagram.

> **Quick Tip:** Buying your first financed car is a big deal because you're going to make payments on a new or certified pre-owned car and actually be held responsible for doing so. As a first time buyer, you are either about to make or break your credit. My biggest piece of advice is: do not just show up to a car lot with hopes and wishes for a decent deal. **You make the deal a decent deal before you show up at the dealership**. It may sound crazy; but when buying a car, the last place you want to go is to a car lot or dealership. The first place you would want to go is to your place of banking. (If you don't have a bank, you should probably only be looking for a cash car.)

What you want to do is have a good idea of how much money you can spend on a car note, weekly gas expenses, timely maintenance (oil change, tire rotations, fuel injections, etc.). Research these numbers for the type of model car you think you can afford. Work out a preliminary budget. Go to whichever financial institution you have; or, that a family member can suggest that will offer you the **lowest interest rate** on a car loan (usually you can research general rates online).

It's easier to get a loan from a financial institution if you have an established relationship with them. Based on your credit, income, and whether or not you have a stable co-signer, the financial institution will tell you upfront how much of a loan you qualify for. By doing this, you have more bargaining power when you do arrive at a dealership. You can also more closely estimate what make and model car you can afford upfront and avoid going over the personal budget that you have already set for yourself. By doing this first, you also save hours you would have spent at the dealership trying to get approved on the spot. **BUT, if at any chance you can get a well-running cash-car I would say go for it; not having a car note could be to your advantage (savings wise).**

If you grind hard to get your guns up; then you don't have time or money to spend on butter that will literally melt.

For example, a car's value depreciates 15-20% a year on average; after one year, a $20K car has only $16K in market value and you will probably still be on the hook for $18K when that year ends, meaning you owe more than the car is worth! As minorities, we need to be souped-up for "survival and war"; and rims (aka butter) can't win any battle. Guns win battles. Let me reiterate what constitutes guns today: something that is, or will yield you cash or power, i.e. real estate, stocks/investments, and/or your ability to leverage your or other's skills and understanding (in the form of some sort of business); or constructing a bartering system.

Our culture lives and breathes the promotion of "butter." A throwback example of this, in hip hop in particular, is the TV series *MTV Cribs*. Back in the day, a rapper knew they had "made it" when they were featured on an episode of *Cribs*. Well the only episode worth watching is the one that features rapper Red Man of Wutang. He later explained in a couple of interviews, not related to the show, that the producers of the show saw his real home and then told him that he should rent a mansion just for the show. He refused to do so. The house he premiered was modest to say the least; but he kept it real. Most times, even when you got a little fame, you can't afford to live in massive opulence, and there's no need to front at the expense of your own livelihood.

Basic Budgeting Skills

The following are two real issues we should all address and work to reconcile:

Having more bills than income:

If you find yourself in this situation, understand that you're going to have to get a little creative and put in some work (meaning a lot of extra effort). Having more bills than income usually results in the "robbing Peter to pay Paul" game. (I repeat that getting out of this situation will take extra effort. A PayDay loan is probably not the best way to solve the problem—that's like selling yourself into modern day slavery.)

You might have to pick up that second or third job/shift, temporarily, just to reestablish on-time full payments of all your financial obligations. The key thing will be to look at all your bills and their due dates. Write them down on one of those big wall calendars so that you can see them every day.

This is when the juggling act comes into play. You need to prioritize! Understand what bills **need** to be paid (especially those that will hit your credit or literally leave you in the dark) and what bills can **wait** (or be paid in partial payments). For example, most bills you have aren't reported on your credit report, at least not until the bill collector sends the unpaid balance to a debt collector—which they usually don't do until months after the original due date—after several attempts are made via phone calls and mailed invoices and/or emails.

The reason original creditors don't go to debt collectors so quickly is because secondary debt collectors make their money by buying your debt from the original creditor for a smaller price than what you owed (probably 25-50% less than your original bill depending on how old the debt is). Then, these bastards (the debt collectors) call you to collect the entire original amount. You can usually come to payment agreements with debt collectors for far less than they ask you for. You must request written proof from a debt collector if you reach a deal with them and pay your account off because they will keep it on your credit report. Some will even come back and ask you for more money.

Now the usual priority of survival may flow as follows (depending on your situation): rent, car, lights, water, lines of credit (credit cards), phone, entertainment subscriptions (Hulu, Netflix, cable, etc.). Know that if you're struggling and you know this ahead of time (i.e. budgeting), you can setup partial payments with all of them. While keeping the service on—or, you can decide to cut them off and just pay off your debt. It is best to call ahead of time (before the bill is due), tell a brief professional synopsis of your situation, make it clear that you want to make a payment, but state that you can only pay half (or whatever percentage you can) of the bill this month.

Just know that for the most part, if a utility company took a deposit from you, if you miss a payment, they are less likely to disconnect you immediately. But you should definitely call and set up a payment plan. Regarding those "unnecessary" bills (strictly entertainment like cable, Netflix, satellite radio subscription, etc.) learn how to bargain; call the cable/phone company like you're going to cancel your subscription, see just how fast they offer you a cheaper deal; especially if you quote them what a competitor is willing to offer for a cheaper price.

Knowing that your bill collectors are willing to work with you on some things within reason, this knowledge coupled with your efforts to grind and pick up that 2nd or 3rd job/shift in addition to developing a (legal) side hustle, you should be able to catch up in no time. Mind you, if you can pay all your bills do so, don't get caught up in this "I'm behind mess," you will only fall deeper in a hole.

Not making the small sacrifices to do better:

The biggest tip would be to practice restraint materialistically. Get rid of the Jordan shoes and/or the name brand purse fetish. Take that money and find a way to flip it legally. Invest in yourself and community; find someone on the same tip, partner up and educate yourselves on investing and cultivating a larger mindset about money. Get together and go over your budgets and goals monthly, if possible. Encourage one another.

A basic budget of your monthly income should look something like this:

- Housing   35%

- Life Necessities   25% (food, health/medicine,   clothes, etc.)

- Debt repayment   15% (if you don't have any debt, you can redistribute this money into savings/investment)

- Transportation   15% (car maintenance, gas, bus/train, etc.)

- Savings   10%

The percentages are generic, and represent the proportion of your monthly income that should be attributed to each spending category. But these percentages will vary based on your particular situation. Bottom line, you have to find what works for you and stick with it.

Learn more about retirement. Heck, try to find a way to retire early. I mean, who wants to be punching a clock for somebody else until your 60+? While you're doing all this, GET READY FOR THE HATE. So many times, other people can get into your head and will down talk you because you may consider something other than what they are doing. For example, one of my personal goals is to retire before 36. I either get two reactions; most people (older) just respond with a laugh and a, "you'll see." (This is usually coupled with a hint of sarcasm.) Others are interested in how I plan on doing it; and offer a bit of encouragement.

Now by retire, I mean to not punch a clock for anyone other than myself. Time is money; and I'm tired of giving my time to others who don't care about me. So, I have to simply be able to make enough money to substitute my current salary. When speaking this out loud, I even have close friends hitting me with the ever so sarcastic, "Good luck with that." But, I had to realize that their vision isn't the same as mine.

Finally, you should have a goal to take the money that is available to you and start reinvesting for self, not in another millionaire. You have to start breaking some long held bad habits with money—many of which have been passed down through your family. Honestly, to make a change for the better, your friends will be the least of your worries, your family will probably question you and put you down more than any other group of people simply because they don't understand. KEEP IT MOVING! You have a goal and a purpose!

Ratchet Financial Behavior Case Study:

I have set this section aside for a special highlight of "Dumb-ass-ness." As scarce as money is, you will continue to find people that find ways to piss it off when they do come up on it. One person in particular that has managed to disappoint me has been Marie Holmes of North Carolina. [Please Google her full story.] This chick needs to be committed. This struggling single black parent won $188 Million Jackpot only to pay $21 Million to post bail like three times for her drug dealing boyfriend (I would say alleged; but this is like the 20th time he's been caught) ☺. Trust me ladies, ain't nothing that good to pay for somebody's bail; especially when they are just dragging you down. To top it off, she ended up going to jail because of her involvement with him.

Original Designer Label

Formed by the one WHO hung the stars:

Such an individual, I individually have the only fingerprint significant enough for me—more secure than any signature you may try to counterfeit. A misfit is far from the truth because my-fit is the shit!

GOD molded my soul, conjured from old—my mother's-mother's-mother's blood runs deep. Deeper than most, deeper than most of you can see, touch, feel… yeah I'm that real!

Loved from HIGH, God put that wonder, that passion in my eye. See y'all on that follow the leader type deal, that road so tired and weathered replete; why don't y'all retire that defunct mindset?

A system sold to you void of advance, that leaves you happenstance, empty hands, and no land… sinking capital, mediocre education in need of complete revocation. Institutionalized religion handed down from slave-master to slave, no face to save; no true paths paved.

Just time wasted, priorities in disarray: selfies and likes from people who ain't even yo friend, only a claim to be true to the end. Add that to a mound of designer labels that ain't able to support yo kids... nothing to pass down to the ghetto babies who feed on the dream of big houses and candy painted whips.

Now I know I'm steppin' on some toes right now

You feel uncomfortable right now... like,

"Who is this chick to read my shit? See, I worked hard for this swag, sold my soul for this bag, stood in line for these J's with my very last pay—to floss like a boss, while still working minimum wage!"

See, my issue ain't with you, but with the system they sold to you. Everybody wanna be different, be that next It, but still rockin' that same ol' shit. Michael Kors this, coach bag that, Louis duffle, y'all niggas look like those old tuxedoes, you know the ones with the ruffles—PLAYED OUT.

See Michael Kors ain't nothing but the new Tommy, Coach ain't nothing but over-priced Guess while y'all out here trying to out dress the rest. And the ones you've made your masters stay paid up.

Got that retail junkie feening, on high waiting for his or her next buy. You oughta be tired of the lie.

Recognize. My individuality ain't marked by no locality—no hood, no school, no membership—no sorority, no designer price tag swinging from a bag, no brand emblem resembling the trees they hung us from! See my blood marks that ancient fit, all natural shit—**the original designer label.**

Your style is what you make it.

Business Focus

In the black community we have marginalized the importance of business ownership, especially in regards to our #YBAs. Your parents may preach over and over again that you need to go to school. Why? To get a "good" education. Why? To get a "good" job. Well, who benefits the most from the job that you work? The owner of the business, right? 9 times out of 10, this person doesn't look like you; nor do they live in the same neighborhood as you. He/she probably goes home to a family, where I can guarantee you that they are not telling their kids to get a "good" education, then get a job! Trust me, that ain't how it works for them.

Throughout my years in college, I have met white business men that start and run business operations that they have not been trained or properly educated in. They just see a need or hole in the market and fill it by using other people that are educated experts—the very same educated experts that your parents/teachers may be pushing you to be.

But at some point, that entrepreneurial spirit has to kick in for us. African Americans were projected by the Nielsen Company to have a spending power of $1.1 Trillion in 2015 (Estimated at $1.7 Trillion by 2017). The reality is that we should be producing enough young black entrepreneurs to tap into our own cash flow; instead of giving it away so frivolously. As a #YBA, you can and should let your money make money! We as black people should make more of an effort to patron black businesses. According to the NAACP, the black $ only circulates within the black community for 6 hours! That's crazy! That literally means once we get our pay checks our money is gone!

Read the article "Does a $ spent in the black community really stay there for only 6 hours?" by Brookie Madison

There is a great importance in being a business-minded person and exploring options of owning your own full-scale or part-time business. Of course, you may have to start small with a home-based side business that may be self-financed. It's called being a hustler. Think about starting it, even right now. If you start a small business in high school, you begin to create your own résumé! When someone asks you do you have experience, you can answer that you run your own business. Besides, making money shows ingenuity and initiative. I'm not saying not to get a conventional job. I'm saying that you can let that job fund your life, business, and passions if you play it the right way; reinvest your paychecks into yourself.

I can't talk about this sense of business orientation that needs to occur in young black America without recognizing the great rise of the Black Wall Street in Tulsa, Oklahoma.

Please Google this subject and write down a couple of facts that are most important or amazing to you.

_____

_____

_____

_____

_____

_____

With all that this city accomplished, it hasn't found a significant place in any of our history books. It was the first city in America to be bombed by air. And guess by who… the American Government! Right-wing radicals always want to talk about how the poor or disenfranchised AKA blacks, Mexicans, and other minorities need to pull themselves up by their boot-straps; time and time again this was done. White America has jealous-heartedly destroyed, no a better word would be TERRORIZED, those that have done just that. Maybe they felt that it in some way threatened their sense of racial superiority (Kanye shrug). So the next time somebody brings up Pearl Harbor or 911 talk about the first air strike of Black Wall Street and see how quiet they get. But, I digress.

Did the story of black ingenuity (minus white hate) spark some kind of enthusiasm? What can you see yourself starting as a business around? The answer: Almost anything. Write a children's book, create an app for the phone, be the candy-man at school, if you braid or cut hair start documenting; or just fully engage in something that you have a true interest in and/or can do really well.

Don't know what you want to do? What interests you? Start thinking completely outside of the box for trades. Begin to look at areas that have very few minorities. NACIS (North American Industry Classification System) codes for minority business owners! [See Non-Traditional Route for further explanation on NACIS codes.] Why should you do this? If you can get in and learn a business that minorities don't have large stakes in, there are opportunities to partner with established similar businesses and get large dollar city, state, and federal contracts. Do you know what that means? $$$ The government is throwing money away left and right anyway, you should establish a business and perfect a craft that they will support and buy from, then redistribute that wealth in your neighborhood. It's a win-win situation if you can learn from an established business and they can help expand your minority business.

FYI school won't give you all the answers when trying to get ventures like these accomplished. I graduated with a

Bachelors of Business Administration (BBA) in entrepreneurial management, but didn't even know how to fill out a business incorporation form for a LLC (Limited Liability Company), LP (Limited Partnership), or even a DBA (Doing Business As) until after I graduated and did my own personal research. I gained more business insight through joining MLM structured businesses and acquired invaluable training [research various MLM companies and how they work].

Boss Status: Don't be an employee and consumer all your life

Let me start off by saying, that owning your own shit makes a big difference in life! For some reason we love to buy buy buy; as it seems that consumerism has completely consumed us. When you live for the weekend, just to hit the mall up, it kind of dries up potential savings to launch a business where customers can line up to throw money at you. It also takes away time you could have spent developing the next best phone app or whatever million dollar ideas you have rolling through your head.

You can have your own hustle right out of school: can you perform a personal service, draw pretty well, have great organizational skills, etc.? People will pay for your services; and in cash too! Don't have a particular skill yet? Become a notary republic (if you have no criminal record), it's easy. All you have to do is pay for and pass the class (which you can then write-off on your taxes), and then file a DBA. Save money to buy a lawn mower or borrow one and cut grass during the summer (file for a DBA, get some business cards printed for literally $10). Registering your DBA is done either with your county clerk's office; or, with your state government, depending on where your business is located. There are a few states that do not require the registering of fictitious business names. Becoming a business owner in Dallas, Texas literally costs $26.

Take that free tax class with one of the big companies like Jackson Hewitt, H & R Block, or Liberty Tax. Work for them for one or two tax seasons then start your own tax service on a personal referral basis. You just created revenue on your own time, under your own circumstances (you make your own hours). It's that easy!

Start looking up the different business structures you could form. Research how to format a business plan (a great tool to attract investors), talk to actual small business owners in your neighborhood. I know that the legality and newness of it all can be overwhelming and may pose huge obstacles, but the point is to start something no matter how small it may sound now. Understand that you don't have to start a multi-million dollar corporation off-bat; Facebook started in a college dorm room. Black people have ways of making something out of nothing so a lack of resources shouldn't be a deterrent.

The most vital resource you have right now is time. There's no way you should ever be bored. If you find yourself bored, it means that you're not serving your brain the amount of stimulation it needs. **You should always be actively living an idea**. Y'all are out here sleeping on basic resources afforded to you in everyday life; especially in terms of technology. Beyonce and Niki Minaj shot the entire "Feelin' Myself" video on an iPhone. People turn into web-celebs through YouTube videos going viral everyday (example Auntie Fee, Phillip & Emmanual Hudson, etc.). You also have numerous ways to get paid for whatever service you can provide, i.e. PayPal, the Square, and other payment apps that can operate on a phone and/or tablet.

Save money, with the purpose of starting some kind of hustle (a small business). Make a goal to put a certain amount back; then, get a loan for that same amount! Now you have doubled the amount of capital at your disposal. (Don't use your own $ if you don't have to.) For those of you that are iffy about getting a loan, think about it this way: it's better to have a line of credit already available for you before you get in a pickle and not have it. Depending on the type of business structure you start, you can go to vendors/suppliers and ask for special terms for billing for the supplies and/or services they grant you. For example, some vendors allow you to pay your invoice to them 30 days after they deliver to you. This gives you some lead time in coming up with the money. Hopefully during that 30 days, you can flip what they have given you, have enough to pay your invoice on time, and have made a profit to reinvest in your business.

You have to think about yourself as a brand and, as a business (beware of social media and putting yourself out there in a negative light. Know that employers and possible partners in business can check your profile, even if it's private). You don't want to put something out there that somebody can screenshot then ruin you years later. Again, develop the ability to talk to people (in a courteous manner), learn to ask for what you need (be clear and precise) in phone conversations, especially via written communication like texting and email. Think about how easily instructions can be misconstrued in person; distant communication can break down and go the wrong way even quicker if the two parties aren't on the same page.

WATCH WHAT YOU SAY TO OTHERS! DON'T LET ANYONE KILL YOUR DREAMS JUST BECAUSE THEY CANT SEE YOUR VISION; IT'S YOUR VISION FOR A REASON! I have a special place for Shaq because I found myself almost being one of those dream killers trying to stick someone into a box of capability. Of all people, the person I almost did this to was my nephew, but then Shaq stopped me. See my nephew has a boatload of ideas (because he's a baby and the world hasn't beaten him down) and loves sports and the thought of helping other people. When I asked him what he wanted to be when he grows up he told me a famous basketball player or a football player, a lawyer if that doesn't work out, and a firefighter and own his own business.

In my grown up closed-mind, I almost said "boy you can't do ALL of that"; but then, I thought of Shaq. Now this was around the same time that Shaq had been presented with a P.H.D. Mind you, Shaq was a phenomenal professional basketball player, is a LAPD cop, an owner of several businesses, a great father, and the list goes on. My nephew could very well be the next Shaq and I almost stepped on his dreams with something as small as a few words of negative discouragement.

YouTube: "Bee Sweet Lemonade's Mission to Save the Bees"

(The story of a young black entrepreneur)

Chapter Notes:

_____

_____

_____

_____

_____

_____

_____

_____

_____

_____

_____

_____

_____

_____

_____

_____

_____

Chapter 3: Maneuvering the Legal System While Black

Legal Matters at 18: A "Justice" System, Unjust for Us

Coming of age in such a litigious society can be a scary and overwhelming situation. Being black; and, coming from a background that's not well versed in the law can pose an even more clouded sense of direction. I know that you've heard your parents, aunts, uncles, or any other older black person talk about how the legal system—whether it be criminal or civil—treats blacks unfairly at a distortional rate. What we don't see a lot of are measures to educate #YBAs on how to critically analyze and use legal know-how to protect yourself from being taken advantage of by the system.

First and foremost, you have to be on your Ps and Qs as a black youth. Try to be on the right side of the law. Don't give them the easy out to crucify you. Because you know whenever shit hits the news they will lie anyway—paint #YBAs as the criminal versus the victim. (When I say "they" I don't mean white people in general; as I'm referring to the elusive system of racial discrimination and not so much the outright bigots of today.)

Out of all the advice I've ever heard, the best was, **if you ever get arrested, don't say anything—ask for your lawyer!** I don't care if you don't have enough money to afford a lawyer, call your mama and shut up! Point blank, don't be scared of that holding tank; even if you're in there for a couple of nights. You will get yourself in more trouble trying to explain your innocence, because they will take your story and flip it, trust! More especially, don't trust the police if they want to bring you to the station for questioning; but they have no warrant for your arrest. As soon as you give a statement, you just may turn into their prime suspect and get arrested—I've seen it happen.

Watch *Menace to Society*

(The real one, not the Wayans Brother's parody—which is hilarious in its own right)

Invisible Racism

Sound Track: "F**k tha Police" by NWA

Racism is overtly silent these days when you have poster examples of black people in seemingly powerful positions; and you have the announcement of Harriet Tubman making it rain on the new 20s. White people on a large scale don't believe that racism is rampant. This is simply because it is not their experience! A person's reality is based on their own unique experience. Your experience as a #YBA is totally different from that of a white person's experience in America. So what does this mean? It means, you can talk until you're blue in the face about racism to most white people and they will argue you down that it's the 21st century and that racism isn't that bad; or, that it doesn't exist at all. This is largely because they themselves have not experienced it.

You have to realize what's happening here. Because your experience doesn't match their experience, they discount you and invalidate your opinion in their head and/or aloud. It's funny how most people will accept a notion about a different group of people; especially if that notion is negative. White people on a large scale do this all the time.

For example, most white people don't believe that black people are harassed unjustly; or that, America has a systematic racist undertone. But, they will believe that black people have natural criminal inclinations more so than white people. This is bullshit! Literally and statistically speaking.

I've been in situations where I have been explaining to a room full of white women what the average black man goes through in dealing with authorities and they respond with a million reasons why the black man could have been doing wrong. In one particular situation, my viewpoint wasn't substantiated until one of the white women actually described a situation where she had helped a co-worker from being harassed by authorities simply by her presence in accompanying him on official business. Her coworker explained how security at the car entry gate usually stops and harasses him on a regular basis and how having a white woman in the car changes that. At this point, the women finally accepted my plight (only after the other white woman validated me).

As a society, we get into dangerous territory when we start to discount a **human experience**. You see, once white people discount and invalidate you and your family's experience it's easy to place you in the category of an extremist, being overly sensitive; or (my fav), they call you a racist for even insisting that such matters are as deep as you assert. In a legal setting, this is done by criminalizing every attribute of your culture. [Please Google & YouTube the work of Jane Elliott.]

The stop and frisk policy in New York is the perfect example of this. It's a policy where the police can stop you for wearing suspicious clothing; equaling baggy pants, hoodies, etc. That's every black teenager on the street. Imagine what would happen if the Department of Justice (DOJ) was out on the street looking for money launderers and the typical dress was a tailored suit… every white man on Wall Street would be "righteously" stopped and frisked; as I'm sure forensic audits would find millions of dollars that have grounds for investigation, but I digress.

The criminalization of the black community is getting out of control. Most recently, we've seen this agenda pushed in the "school to prison pipeline." How are they continuing this method of criminalizing #YBAs in school? It is accomplished by punishing, expelling, and trying to humiliate black kids because of their **hair**! Google stories about Vanessa VanDyke (of Florida), Teresa Quansah (of Toronto), RaShaad Hunter (of Alabama), Tiana Parker (of Oklahoma), and Isaiah Freeman (of Virginia).

Several A-honor roll black kids have been suspended for the 1st time because they wear their hair in its naturally curly state. It's utterly ridiculous to criminalize a #YBA because of the way God decided their hair should grow. But, it simply goes deeper than their hair creating a "distraction" for the class.

You see, when you take a young child and begin to condition that child into thinking that everything about them is wrong, even the way that their hair grows, you start to break their spirit and the love that they have for themselves. Everybody knows that it's easier to break the spirit of a child than a grown man or woman who knows who they are. When you begin to break the confidence in a child, you begin to negatively shape their self-image. Now, we're right back to those plantation type tactics "Masta" used and perfected.

YouTube: "Leo Muhammad: The True History of Slavery"

(Pay close attention @ mark 13:30)

At large, white people in our society are taught to look at black people, our culture, our needs, our wants, and our view point in a devoid manner. Once you understand this system, it's kind of hard to be as quick tempered about ignorant white people because you begin to see that they really don't get it. This may become frustrating as hell. You can't have their ignorance be your burden! You have so much more to focus your energy on.

A prime example of this is the #BlackLivesMatter movement. No sooner than the hashtag was birthed, it was aborted and charted as a stillbirth by mainstream white America; countering with #AllLivesMatter. As black people, we all probably sat in front of the TV, or an online blog, shaking our heads and cursing, "Dumb asses. We know all lives matter; but y'all don't seem to understand that black lives are included in that!" This is because mainstream America doesn't understand or care that for most black people, in these times, it seems to be a blessing to survive a god damn traffic stop without getting shot! [Please Google info on personal dash cams you can buy that can upload video from your car to a memory card or online. This way you don't just have the cops' video to prove their unjustified behavior (which they cut and tamper with).]

We as black people already understand the harshness with which we are treated by the justice system. From most blacks, initial contact with the police on the street is a life threating experience; and, harsher sentencing practices within the judicial process are a guarantee if you are arrested and charged. Once we are lunged into the system, we have no chance of a productive life in mainstream society after prison (verses the second and third chances granted to our white counterparts).

Log on to <u>www.crimingwhilewhite.com</u> to examine self-reported white privilege

---

When it comes to the issue of police brutality and confrontation, all I can say to our #YBAs is, "Do whatever it is that you must do to stay alive at the end of the day." Sadly, there is nothing else that can be said; especially when your life is in the hands of someone that doesn't care about you. Knowing that even if you do everything by the book, someone with "authority" can still take your life deeply saddens me, even more so because I, **WE**, as a community haven't found the answer to this reoccurring situation.

I googled a million articles on the things a black person should do when they encounter the police; and none of them seemed significant enough to mention. None of the articles seemed to have given enough information that the parent of Tamir Rice could have passed on to their child to stop a white cop from shooting him dead on the playground.

What burdens my heart the most is that I look at my little nephew and nieces and the high school mentees and wonder over and over again, what I can tell them that might save their lives if they were in the same situation. Then I start to think, "Well shit, what would I do if it were me? What would stop a cop from shooting me no questions asked? The answer: Nothing probably; especially if the cop knows the shooting will be ruled 'justified' SMH."

YouTube "Professor James Small speaks on the history of cops and Gangs" (50:57)

(Sheds a very detailed historical light on how dirty the "cop business" really is and how they use policy to entrap black men into felony convictions on a daily basis)

Money and control: After the Dead Bodies Pile up

One hundred and fifty years after the last slave catcher has retired, the system is still buying and selling black bodies. Cops in the street shoot us down, the county then takes possession of our bodies, and the selling of our organs are commenced. After some bullshit ass autopsy is reconfigured in favor of the shooter's story, a news report is released to the public.

One story in particular that has sat on my heart is the story of Kendrick Johnson. [Please Google for full story.] In 2013, his body was found rolled up in a gym mat behind the bleachers at his school, Lowndes High, in Georgia. An original autopsy (done by local officials) concluded that he died from accidental position asphyxia. The family paid for an independent autopsy which reported significantly different findings. First of all, any lay person looking at Kendrick's after death photo can tell he was badly beaten. The independent autopsy found the death to be caused by blunt force trauma. But the bigger issue was that upon the independent autopsy, Kendrick's body was opened up only to find it stuffed with newspapers!

All his internal organs were missing (no doubt sold on the black market). [Sale of organs on the black market is a real thing; especially the sale of African—melanin carrying—organs, which carry a greater dollar value. Google the story of UCLA being sued for the selling of cadaver's organs.] They claimed that his internal organs were destroyed and discarded by the prosecutor before the body was sent back to Valdosta. This was allegedly done without the family's consent.

To add insult to injury, the Georgia Secretary of State's Office cleared all handlers of Kendrick's body of any wrongdoing and the FBI concluded that his death was an accident with no foul play. This was done even in light of a forensic analyst, enlisted by CNN, findings that tapes from two cameras of the school's surveillance were missing an hour and five minutes of footage. The sad part is that there are countless other incidents like this story that occur every day; more in my city of Dallas than I would like to hear.

YouTube: "John Steward on Baltimore & the Police Brutality Lotto"

Analyst of the Freddie Gray story paints a more vivid picture of the palm-greasing technique the "justice" system uses to maintain its ability to kill at will. [Please Google full story.] Freddie Gray was arrested because he started running when he saw the police. On paper, he was detained for having a switchblade (which later was determined to be a legal knife). Police handcuffed him after putting him in a tactical hold and denying him his inhaler. He was then transported in a police van. At some point during his transport (while in handcuffs and leg irons), he obtained injury to his head; and his spine was 80% severed at the neck. Who knows what the hell, or should I say who the hell in blue, happened to Freddie, I know one thing, the $6.4 Million wrongful-death settlement his family received can't bring him back.

In a 2014 case, a California Highway Patrol officer repeatedly punched a 51 year old black woman in the face after he wrestled her to the ground for walking within traffic lanes. [Please Google full story.] Marlene Pinnock received a $1.5 Million settlement for her harassment and beating. Here we have $ exchanging hands while officers get a slap on the wrist; but no policy changes seem to occur—no death sentences have been sought in response of those that have lost life. With these numerous occurrences within the black community, the system seems to be anything but "just."

The 20th anniversary of the million man march just occurred on Oct. 9th and 10th of 2015; and we still have a laundry list of black victims that have died at the hands of the police and white men on the street that think they are the police. The march is still needed, how much progress has really occurred? After another black unarmed male is shot we have a march and/or a riot. The system continues to take our lives with bullets, assault, and unjustified prison sentences [Google the Innocence Project and payment schedules for exonerated prisoners]; then, throws a couple of dollars in hush money. But our time is priceless! We need to begin to react to these wrongs in a manner more influential than a march. [Please YouTube "MSNBC: story of Jared Adams."]

Taking off the Rose Colored Glasses: History of US Justice System

---

Read *The New Jim Crow* by Michelle Alexander

As African-Americans, and other minorities in general, we are taught within our families and churches that the justice system isn't fair. The news amplifies this; and throws it in our face every time a not-guilty verdict for a white person that has murdered an unarmed black person airs in the headlines. We know the system is unfair. We protest (alongside some semi-conscious or guilt-burdened white people) while a large majority of right-wing white folks yell out that we are just sensitive; and are using the race card.

As teens, you may be caught in the conceptual idea that this is the way it is; and it will always be this way because that's just what you have been told. My objective in this section is to highlight some of the larger reasons and systematic schemas present in the "justice" system to give you a little more insight into the system; and why it is the way it is (all the real stuff that they ignore in your bullshit government classes).

My point in this segment is to expose the systems design, in its natural form, to sustain the slave system. [Please see and read Appendix A.] You need to know and fully comprehend that pretty much every single decision you make on a daily basis effects not only you; but those around you (friends and family) and those people that haven't even entered your life yet (future spouses and kids). This message goes out especially to my young black boys (because we all know that the system is gunnin' for you like target practice—literally).

Getting in legal trouble, especially early in life, can lead to an uphill battle in trying to succeed financially and socially. Collecting felony charges can hinder your chances of getting financial aid for college or trade school, knock you out of contention for certain jobs; and even have an effect on who you can marry (most people in government, law enforcement, and banking can't get married to felons).

Finding yourself in a life altering legal situation is easier than you could ever imagine, EVEN IF YOUR INNOCENT! Guilt by association is one of the most common ways a black person gets caught up (besides the frequently mistaken identity scenario, because white people think we all look alike). Just for a second, imagine your friend ask you to ride to the corner store with them. You agree. When you get there, you realize that they were going up to someone you didn't know to buy some weed (in a non-recreational state); or, some pills or whatever new thing people find to get high off of. Three seconds later, the police pop up.

Guess what? You're going to jail! It doesn't matter that you didn't know what your friend was doing, you are going to jail with them; and the worse part about it was that you're so-called friend got you into a bad situation that fast.

A situation occurred a few years back in Dallas. Two young black males were signaled by a cop to pull over. Well, the driver refused and started a chase. He sped into an apartment complex, jumped out of the car, fled on foot, and left the passenger in the car. A white female cop approached the car with her gun drawn, told the passenger to put his hands up and proceeded to shoot him in the same breath.

Now as I watched the dash cam video, the 1st question in my head was, why didn't the passenger hop out with the driver and run? Well later on after the situation was assessed, the police found out that the driver stole the car; then hours later, picked up the passenger (who didn't know that the car was stolen). The passenger stayed in the car because he didn't know what the hell was going on. What was his consequence? He got shot!

It was obvious from the tape that the officer was wrong for shooting so quickly; especially since the boy actually put his hands up as she requested. The officer was later fired; but look at how jacked up the situation was. The passenger actually lived; but to think, his "homeboy" put him in that position without any remorse.

As you get older, you will see that people don't think twice about getting you involved in their bullshit! Just look at how easily you may find yourself in some mess at school; or even in your family just because somebody wanted some attention, started flexin' and threw your name into some gossip, whether true or false. It only gets messier as you get older. Drake made the comment in the song "Energy" that his circle is getting so small it's looking like a period. That happens for a reason. My mama told my brother the truest statement, "Your 'circle' of friends needs to be a 'C,' so you can let some of them snakes out." Some people you are going to have to grow out of as you move through different stages and evolve (mentally, emotionally, and spiritually).

Understand that it's bigger than avoiding jail and prison. You have to look at the system and what it represents. Look at how many black people are under the control of the "justice" system via probation, parole, the paying of retribution and the families paying for inmates' upkeep (via commissary).

It's not fair that our #YBBs (young black boys) don't get the chance to fully experience ,their childhood because it's a system out here—called "justice"—that continually puts them in a grown man's position. I have personally had conversations with my adolescent nephew that I know has probably scared him—robbing him of a bit of his innocence every time another "incident" with an unarmed black male comes up. Or, when something happens to him at school and he just feels like everyone is coming for him and he doesn't understand why. But I, and the members of my family, know that if we don't keep it **100** with him; then he's going to be blindsided on the street in a situation he may not be prepared for, right? I mean, look at the case of 14 year old George Stinney Jr. [Google full story].

Watch the movie Kill the Messenger &

Freeway: Crack in the System

(Both chronicle the story of infamous dealer Rick Ross—not the rapper—and shows how the US C.I.A. used him to funnel crack into black communities)

We as black people don't trust the system. It's some kind of innate thing because, for the most part, we all agree something usually doesn't sound right. These hunches are backed more and more as history reveals itself showing how the government has and continues to conspire against us.

I remember finding out about the Tuskegee Syphilis Experiment while in under grad [please Google full story]. Being the only black student in my science lab, the assistant that brought it up in lecture asked me did I know about it (sadly I didn't). Then, I remember finding out about the Black Panther Cointelpro government setup [please Google full story]. Again, being the only black student in this grad class, the professor asked if I knew about it (sadly I didn't).

Years later, I found out that the government openly admitted to killing MLK in a U.S. Civil Court. [Please Google article "Martin Luther King assassinated by US Govt: King Family civil trial verdict."]Then I found out about the government practicing radiation on black kids. [YouTube "Shocking African American Radiation Experiments left holes in American Black Kids Heads.] The most recent attack has been the lead water crisis in majority black neighborhoods in Michigan.

After learning about all of these proven government plots of destroying the black community (comparable to Nazi

Germany, but worse because of the long time span the government has continued to attack us), you quickly learn that survival for us is constantly fought on two ends. We have to compete for survival on a basic level like every other person (food, shelter, and clothing); and then, we have to fight the "invisible" danger that the government poses to us.

It's hard enough being a black person on the right side of the law with all the odds piled against you. The allure of pulling a fast-one and making some money always presents a scratch you want to itch when were desperate to obtain food, shelter, and clothing. It's even easier to scratch that itch when the government hands you a back scratcher.

On a broader scale, you find that the government makes it easier for #YBAs to engage in criminal activity than providing adequate resources for them to build legitimate businesses; or, to constructively grow positive black cultural movements. Rick Ross explicitly laid out how his dreams of aspiring as a college athlete were quickly cut short and how easily he was handed crack via a C.I.A paid international drug dealer. Ross played a pawn in the US Government's ploy to fund a war by sucking funds from poor black neighborhoods in a trade for drugs flown in on government planes. This is no conspiracy theory; as the CIA has released reports admitting to their involvement. [Please read Appendix B for more background on the War on Drugs.]

Let's really evaluate the situation. The government gets to dictate who can do "illegal" activity and those groups who cannot. Look at the drug game—because all it truly is, is a game. Who's one of the most notorious drug dealers you know?

Did you just name a person off the streets? Because off the top of my head, I came up with the top five pharmaceutical companies in America (Johnson & Johnson, Pfizer, Abbott Labs, Bristol Myers, Squibb, and Amgen). Most of their merchandise has more negative side-effects than crack or heroine; but their "legal" business brings in big revenues.

116

Now the biggest local drug dealer you know has a post (or corner) at every intersection in a middle class area. Starbucks has got the biggest lock on **corner drug sells!** Let's get it straight, caffeine is a drug (in a technical sense it's a substance that has a physiological effect when ingested).

These bean slinging thugs are at every corner; and have no conscience about who they expose their products to—adults, teenagers, and adolescent kids, alike. The caffeine epidemic is getting out of control. They have people strung-out, fiending for a high; and millions of individual drinkers late for work just to stop by the "trap" drive-through, spending ridiculous amounts of their income. It's no telling who and how many politician coalitions and grass root organizations they have "ganged up" in order to lobby and run the streets (via the legislative system). [YouTube the documentary "The Corporation (2003)" (2:24:03 in length)]

How does that sound? Somewhat like how the media uses language to characterize a street dealer? The system paints a villain through selective choice; it punishes scapegoats for selling a harmful product that the system itself puts on the street in the first place (i.e., automatic weapons, cocaine, heroin, etc.).

Now imagine if black folks on the street were able to legally package and sell weed on the corner (from a depreciable permanent post/building)... oh my bad, white folks have now coined that industry with "distilleries!" Funny that these "legal" distilleries sell weed that contains more artificial chemicals than the average weed sold on the streets back in the day—when a brotha would end up serving an exaggerated sentence for 10 to 20 years.

But then again, how can you expect for the legal system to serve you any justice when the whole system is rigged: judicial, legislative, and executive. Society won't ever admit to the conspiracy; as they persecute the honest, calling them crazy, labelling them as conspiracy theorists. But, at what point do the facts-on top-of-facts prove the obvious cover up?

The Other Side of the Coin

Now let's get off the innocence boat and take some ownership in the problem; aside from the extremely visual injustices of the legal system. You make it easier for them (the corrupt systematic "justice" tool) when you play into the hands of said system. Some things we can only blame on ourselves because we know how the system is set up and how it will play us; but for a lack of a better phrase, "we still do some stupid shit!" Sadly, because of the construct of our legal system, jail and/or prison is basic part of our black community (i.e. referred to as "university" for our men).

When you think of school, you think of a gathering place where family and friends have had life changing moments that have elevated them to the next level. Back in the day, it wasn't uncommon for entire families to have graduated from the same high schools; or, for kids to follow in their parents footprints and attend the same college as their parents. It used to be a black parent's pride to announce that their child is attending their HBCU alma mater.

Well, in the black community; especially amongst those of us in the lower economic rungs, this tradition of the prison "university" is real and is getting a little old. For example, my little brother has been serving a sentence now for the last six years or so. On multiple occasions during visits to see him, he has updated me on people close to us that ended up not only in prison; but in the very same prison as him—even in the same cell as him.

It's crazy when your little brother tells you that he ended up sharing a cell with your former step-dad, SMH ☹. Or, that your old elementary classmate is serving time in the same prison for Lord knows what (I think he told me murder or a violent crime). Or, that y'all childhood neighbor is in the same prison and just served 7 years for armed robbery of a convenience store. It was the "university" that brought them all back to the same place.

Just like everything else in this Westernized section of the world, money is the object of the game and generations of #YBAs are at the backbone of the money scheme when it comes to prison. Everything from the phone call you make, to the commissary you buy, to the email you send someone in prison, you pay the cost, plus a premium fee. This game is something else because if they don't get you to buy into consumerism (to spend your $ in their corporate stores); then they get you to spend exorbitant amounts in fees to the prison system to keep your loved one afloat.

Having a loved one in jail or prison is like being imprisoned yourself; especially during a visit. I have personally had to make that trip more times than I would have liked. I still dread the early mornings that I have to get up to visit my brother (four hours away). The personal search during a maximum security visit sucks! It sucks even more to come for a visit and have to break bad news to a family member that's locked up. For some reason, you feel guilty for telling them news that you know is going to break them down.

I don't think that our family members who actively get into trouble realize the sacrifice we have to make until they have spent a ridiculous amount of time behind bars.

Sound Track I Ain't Mad At Cha by TuPac

For those of you getting released from imprisonment, there are no excuses in getting your life back on track! Grind after Prison! You have to be ready (mentally and emotionally) to reinvent yourself from nothing. But for my #YBAs, don't even put yourself in this position in the first place.

The choice is yours (to the extent of injustice). Every day, you have the individual choice to make "good" or "bad" choices. These choices will either positively contribute to your life or negatively contribute to your life. One of those first set of choices starts with the company you keep AKA "yo friends."

"Show me your friends and I'll show you your future"

-John Kuebler

This statement reigns true. We all know that it's harder to get into trouble by yourself. Even if you do something bad, you know that you won't snitch on yourself. Now if you're running with a crew, the show *48 Hours* chronicles how that usually goes down. But for real, the preservation of black lives is of the utmost important issue; especially involving legal situations. Knowing you rights in your state is the first line of defense you have.

A Letter from Prison

8:55pm   5/11/16

I could've done a couple things different for me to not have come to prison like: #1) follow the law and #2) pay a lil more attention to the advice that was given to me throughout my life by multiple people who cared, loved and tried to help a young black boy that was obviously lost and going in the wrong direction! Now that I'm in prison and have been here for the past 6 years on a ten year sentence, I've adjusted a lot, but at first it was hard!

Being 18 years old and fresh off the streets, I had a real hard problem with accepting authority and being told what to do. Especially by, in my case, a guard that's my age or just a couple of years older, but clearly less intelligent and obviously on a power trip! Or maybe somebody that reminds you of the guy who used to get picked on in middle school and now [sic] is out for vengeance! Sounds funny but that's been my life for the past 6 years.

If you've never been to prison, it's really something that's hard to imagine. You can be told over and over and watch 100 movies but that's honestly not enough! It's hard to explain how being [sic] taken away from "everything" feels: friends, family, food, clothes, sunlight, fresh air, Freedom! I mean everything!

Some situations are worse than others depending on the location and your behavior, but to me it's all the same! If you ain't strong, it'll do the worse to your spirit and brake you all the way down. I done seen people that I knew from the outside that were players, ballers, and gangstas come down here and lose they [sic] mind, literally!

Players lose their hair from stress that's coming from all different directions. Ballers that [sic] are broke and look everything less than "ballin'" cuz they done lost all support from the outside world and can't even get to commissary and buy a 25 cent soup, ain't gangsta (SMH)! You know it's bad when this got men thinking that other men starting to look attractive; it's sad but true.

People kill they self on a daily basis in here. I seen a man layin' dead on the floor not even 10 feet away from me for at least 10 minutes before they came and attempted to give him medical attention! It's scary just thinking about the different risk you take just waking up and making it through the day: from riots where you got 100 people (literally) fighting [sic] all the time with shanks, metal trash cans, and anything that can be used as a weapon; to having to worry about guards that had a bad day at home and had it on his or her mind to come to work and let it out on the first person they see.

And when you an inmate in all white, you're always wrong even when you're right! Having to depend on someone (who doesn't care about your wellbeing) for protection or help (and most times [sic] is your biggest threat) makes it that much harder to be in a good mood or keep a good spirit! Most people just fall right in place with the bullshit, violence, and everything else that ain't productive.

It's hard to be a leader in a place like this and when I say leader I mean someone who leads his own thoughts and actions and not let his situation and surrounding chose for him! I can say that I'm blessed to be able to experience this experience without losing myself. But even more, learning and finding myself. I had to make the choice to change my life by changing my thought process and then my actions. I needed to see firsthand that this ain't how I wanted to spend the rest of my life or any extra years!

Most importantly is what you chose to do with your time. I exercise my mind by reading for the most part and now tryna understand life to the best of my ability. To me, this is the definition of a reality check! I see life in a whole new aspect and having everything taken from me slowly made [sic] me value the small things in life that I was taking for granted, like using the restroom in private, going outside when the sun's out, or even chewing a piece of gum!

I don't know how things will be when I get out, but as for me, one thing I can guarantee is that I will be more patient, humble, appreciative, and dedicated to my goals and morals in life. I feel that I'm ready to get out and put all my plans into action. I took my time and used it at its fullest potential possible. I don't look at life [sic] as just something that I have to do until I die anymore.

I look at life as an opportunity in every direction. I learned what love really was, being around so much hate and what happiness was after being sad for so long. Long story short, I see things for what they really are now and by me still being in prison I'm still learning. And by me learning what I've learned, I'll continue to learn even after I've done time behind prison walls.

I found myself, found my talents, and perfected my craft with the time that I've had to myself. You will find some of the most talented people in prison in almost every category possible: rappers, ball players, book writers, anything you can think of. I even seen somebody make a light bulb out of simple things like paper clips and paper; speakers from cardboard and magnets; tattoo guns from screws and wirers!

Pressure makes diamonds! In other words, sometimes a hard situation will bring out the best in you and that's what prison has done for me and a lot of others who were strong and smart enough to try to turn a problem into a blessing. For any and everybody having a tough time in life, faced with a problem, or just lost and confused, change is possible!

I'm changing every day, step by step, little by little, and you can too. You can do "anything" that you put your mind, body, and soul into regardless [sic] of how bad it looks or how much the odds are against you. Keep your head up. Stay focused and dedicated and make it happen.

James McKellar

AKA Lil Dude

Semantics

Defined as the meaning of a word, phrase, sentence, or text

These politicians be some bandits with these semantics

Fiendish tactics with their ravenous antics

Promises vanish, covered by pragmatic infused panic

Got they constitutes running frantic

Performing gymnastics on the largest platform.

Pulling heart-strings, summing sins with every pike, twist, and spin amidst their dismount into a WIN.

A stolen election.

Never mind the people's insurrection—a rebellion like no other,

Subdued with a confection of government cover-up, conspiracy mastermind hush-up—a sabotage like no other

Bleed the people blue and black then watch their resistance draw back, they say

Feed them another lie my friend then back to the attack

Lull them back to silence with a pill of tyrants—call 'em terrorist that inflict violence

Scare them half to death until they yield compliant.

Change the laws quietly while calming their anxiety

Decrease their sobriety to perpetuate the illusion of a high society

I must say, these politicians be some bandits with these semantics

Fiendish tactics with their ravenous antics

Promises vanish, covered by pragmatic infused panic

Got they constitutes running frantic

THESE SEMANTICS!

YouTube "B.o.B – EARTHQUAKE- Official Video"

Chapter Notes:

Chapter 4: Religion and All Your Unanswered Questions

YouTube "Eddie Griffin on Christians, Muslims, Bible, & Jesus" (this was hilarious)

Ever had a question about God; or your religion? Were you ever bold enough to ask your mama, daddy, or the pastor? What kind of answer did you get? If it didn't sound quite right, did you still just roll with it? This section of the book is not intended to shake anyone's religious foundation; but more so to make you further investigate and understand the need to study your religion while strengthening your spirituality, and understanding the difference in the two.

Let's start with the basics. Write down every single question that you have ever had in your head about religion as you know it. In particular, write down those questions that no one has been able to answer for you. I don't care if the first question is, "Does God really exists?" Write it down.

_____

_____

_____

_____

_____

_____

_____

For some reason, I'm pretty sure it resorts back to slavery, the black community doesn't really support the notion of deep inquisition—the questioning of the status quo—especially as it relates to the religion **given** to us. Have you ever come to a crossroad where you thought that going to church on Sunday and Bible study on Wednesday just wasn't enough? Ever wonder if there was something else you're supposed to do, feel, or know?

As a teen, I would sit in church, listen to the pastor preach a lesson (which seemed to sound just like the one from the month before) that really didn't have much depth (as far as history—the "who," "what," "when," and "where" of the situation). Then someone would yell out "preach Pastor." Then the Pastor would get louder and the choir would play his hype hymn in the background, while the organist and/or drummer hit a couple of cords right on time.

Is this sounding familiar to any of y'all? Then, in the end, it didn't matter what part of the Bible we were in; or who we were talking about, we always ended at Calvary. This all foreshadowed the collection plate cycling around—once, twice, and sometimes three times. (Mind you, I'm not talking down on the church, just sighting my observations.)

I realized I wasn't getting enough information, enough history! I had questions about the faith I claimed to live, breathe, and be reborn in. So I made an extra effort; I started going to bible study at a couple different churches to get the depth I was looking for. That dried up after like 3 months. I was thirsting for this knowledge that I just couldn't seem to get in the church. I started getting deep into some independent study, because the information I was receiving second-hand was watered down and surface level.

Mind you, by this point in my religious journey, I had a couple of college level World Religion classes under my belt. It blew my mind to find how many similarities, morals, even traditions that different religions inside and outside of Christianity have in common. All I had to do was remove the name of the one, or collective deity, a religion claimed as God and all the religions pretty much became fluid. So once I dived into some major independent reading—which more so involved the historical facts of the major 3 religions, I began to cut through the bullshit and started to get to the real.

YouTube Eric Vaugh "I'm Stupid Juiced"

The following was a couple of basic things I started to do when I started my independent search:

- Go online and write down the definition of RELIGION; then, SPIRITUALITY; and then, SCIENCE. What differences/similarities do you find?

- Look in an etymology dictionary online and look up the word RELIGION again.

- Google "similarities of major world religions"? What surprises you the most about some of your findings?

Notes:

_____

_____

_____

_____

_____

_____

_____

_____

Seeing Religion through Certain Understandings
(reflections of my own thoughts):

Watch Documentary *Out of Darkness*

What I found was that there is no difference between science and the true realization of my own spirituality; but, there is definitely a difference between science and religious dogma. All parts of true science (quantum physics, chemistry, astronomy, math, etc.) only further prove that there exists some Divine Manifestation; as there are natural occurrences that replicate exponentially in space, in the human body, in nature that cannot be explained away by pure coincidences. I have always wondered, "What's the big deal between science (the Big Bang) and Creationism (the Genesis story)?" If all these people from different regions, languages, and races have the same morals and ideas about God (no matter the name used), what's the problem?

Through self-research I grew to further understand the true nature of religion as a weapon via warfare, a tool of mind-control; and, its direct correlation with politics and policy. As you move through a journey of reflection and research, you will begin to recognize the glaring similarities and likeness in all major religions. It is extremely important to understand the historical context behind the proliferation of all religions (mainly through political agenda). You have to know history—and not that bland watered-down half-truth stuff taught in school.

You have to fill in the holes with self-education. Once you recognize the similarities of the religions, study more. Be able to pinpoint some of the major differences; and begin to question why these differences exist. Assess who stands to benefit from the differences within each religion. Who gains more social status, political clout, and/or financial gain for certain interpretations in religious text and rules superimposed by religious leaders? Holistically, what begins to surface is that some groups of people will use tenants of religious "law" to take advantage of another group of people.

I also began to look at the large scale whitewashing of all religions; and the Europeanizing of the main figures, along with the changing of their names. For example, in the Bible we go from African sounding names/places to European sounding names and places that supposedly occurred in the same regions.

I also started boldly addressing discrepancies I had within my own religion (Baptist-Christian)—things that just didn't make sense; or sit right in my spirit. Basically, I started addressing those answers to questions I've heard all my life that I was told to believe simply because that was just what faith was. [Look up the definition of faith; not because I don't think you know what it is, but because you should see the literal interpretation of the word and maybe its etymology as well.]

The reasons most of what you have been told doesn't make sense or sit right with you is because most stories are taken out of context and manipulated. Then, when retold, they are further distorted (similar to playing the game "telephone"). In addition, these stories were edited by individuals that didn't truly understand their purpose and meaning in the very 1st place. The stories were reconfigured and used to control the masses.

In the same manner of thought, accurate historical facts and religious timelines never seem to line up: creation vs. evolution; and, biblical stories vs. world history. The entire world has a long line and connection to African origin; and these African ties are directly linked to Biblical characters, genealogy, and places. Yet, the original stories have been muddied and devoid of whole truths. True science dispels lies, though. Archeologist continue to unearth black bodies in Africa that date back thousands to millions of years before the compilation of the bible. Yet, I'm supposed to believe that Adam and Eve were white.

I deduce that the disconnect that exists between the bible and its African ties continues because of the whitewashing and changing of names connected with the adaptation of the African spiritual system that Jews, and non-black converts of Christianity and Islam, insurrected while trying to make their own ties to the spiritual stories. Each of these sects of religion also force their followers to ascribe fully to one "true" story; denying that there could be historical and scientific confirmation of other legitimate spiritual/religious occurrences. I, personally, find it very probable that God sent several prophets to the world at different times in different regions. The message that was sent was generally of the same tenants and lessons; but were tailored to that sect of peoples' culture and time.

My main problem with religion as an "institution" is its reluctance to be wrong; as religion can't seem to be honest about what is just truly unknown. I figure there are many unknowns about the Devine Creator that just aren't for us to understand; things we will never fully grasp because it's too far beyond our comprehension. But when "terrorist" (power thirsty individuals and institutions) claim to know these unknowns and conspire to spread their lies, we as people have to think a little harder as to not follow like mindless sheep. A great truth in history (quantified in historical and scientific evidence) has been covered, manipulated, and forced down the throats of the masses.

I have truly embraced the idea of not allowing anyone to paint God/The Devine/The Creator into a box. For example, my then 6 year old niece told me that she saw a pictures of God; and that he was a white old man with a beard. Well, who says that God is white? Who says that God is a man? Could The Creator just be a combination of both a feminine and masculine energy? Why is God even portrayed as a person? You would think a power as Holy as being the Ruler of all the worlds would look a little different than mere man. But I'm just saying.

Notes/Thoughts:

_____

_____

_____

_____

_____

_____

_____

_____

Fix it White Jesus! (A Fast Food God)

_____

Task: get acquainted with the works of Mr. John Henrik Clarke via YouTube and your local library

_____

Have you ever had fast food so many times in a week that you couldn't wait to get a home-cooked meal? It's probably because fast food consists mostly of fats and sugar; while that home cooked meal delivers an actual substance to your body. Most of us have been digesting a fast food religion, handed to us on a cheap, prepackaged platter. Ever wonder why some people consistently run to the church house, but still can't get right?

#YBAs are all encouraged to go to church, go to bible study, and to know the basic stories of the bible. How many times have you wondered, "Where the black people at?" Has there always been this disconnect between what you "learn" in church, what's taught in school, and what you feel about black people's place in all of this?

You have been taught to "think past color and logic"; where images of white people cloud your vision of ancient biblical people who live in the hottest areas in the world. You are conditioned to think down upon blackness and its assumed association with dark devilish or demonic things. The truth is everything originates from darkness, black, blackness, even the people in the bible.

For so long, they have just been dressed up in white face and served to you in movie form. A perfect example was the latest production of the Exodus taking place in Egypt; with all characters cast as white. The director caught a lot of flak for casting. He even said that he wouldn't have been able to get his movie funded if he casted black actors. How is it that you can't cast black people; especially since Moses blended in with black Egyptians and married an Ethiopian woman (another country in Africa)? For so long, you and your pastors have no idea of what main characters in the bible really looked like and who they really were.

What is your definition of black? What type of connotations or feelings do you associate with being black? You need to understand the truth of black; it is every single color collected in one. This is why nothing can exist without blackness. The bible even tells you that God created light from the darkness. The dark matter in space consists of melanin. Just as pieces of us make up the ever long and distant universe, you are present "all up and through" the bible and in other sacred spiritual text that predates the bible by thousands of years!

YouTube "Blacks in the Scripture: Blacks in the Bible"

(Fair warning, the guy narrating this lecture sounds like the guy from the Clear eyes commercial and is a little lame in his delivery; but, he has some good visualizations and his information is very detailed and eye opening compared to the way you have heard all the bible stories before.)

I've read through several books concerning Buddhism, Hinduism, Zoroastrianism, etc. One of the main ones that kept my attention, so much so that I read the entire book front to back, was *The Complete Idiot's Guide to Islam* by Yahiya Emerick. Off top, this book said that Adam and Eve were black and originated from Africa—my heart could have smiled! Mind you, Yahiya Emerick, the author, is anything but a black man! It was even more shocking to me that somebody other than a religious black man actually admitted to this fact so plainly. Besides the race of the author, I had never seen a "religion" as a whole admit to that; science had, but no religion that I had ever heard of.

Then, as I continued to read, I found that 50-60% of the questions I never had answered through Christianity were being answered through Emericks book! I mean things about God and the world that I had alone conceptualized in my head as true were being confirmed by the things that Islam held as a known truth. For example, I had always equated the Big Bang theory with the story of Genesis and God proclaiming "let there be light."

I always associated the 6 "days" with the timeline of evolution explained through science, in which God created everything from the Earth's crust, to its oceans, to its animals, and then man. Who is man to know exactly how long God's days are anyway? It made sense to me; especially since the actual land (Earth) is so many billions of years older than man, and aquatic life existed before life on the surface of the Earth, and that animals were manifested the "day" before man. That explained to me why dinosaurs were here so many years earlier than man. I didn't understand why religious Christian leaders were so hell-bent on downing scientific evidence.

There was never any conflict in my head that creationism (religion) and evolution (science) couldn't exist in the same spiritual sense; unlike what they try to convince the public of through political agenda. But besides all of this, when I read that the author Emericks was a historian, I had a great appreciation for the information I had received from the book. Now, I didn't agree with everything in the book, but it opened my eyes. The next incident that moved me to my next stage of soul searching occurred a couple of weeks after I finished that book.

I was going through a personal bout of sadness and disappointment. A friend of mine who happened to be a Muslim gave me a Muslim prayer written in English. I carried it around for a week before I actually recited the prayer. By this point, I felt a grave heaviness. So while at work, I closed my office door, fell to my knees and recited this Muslim prayer. No lie, in the same moment I finished the prayer, I felt a sense of peace come over me for literally 2 or 3 minutes (and in a meditative state that's a long time). I mean I had NEVER felt something like this before. It was like without actual words God had told me that I was ok. At that very moment, I truly understood that The Devine knows no "religion," it's bigger than all of that.

I branched out and started studying all major religions. Once I began studying Asiatic religions and the similarities between Jesus and Buddha (via Ivan van Sertims's YouTube lectures), there was no turning back. Buddha was like 300 years older than Jesus; but the similarities between the two were apparent. The more reading and research I did on Buddha, the more I found substantial evidence that original statues (most that out dated Buddhist religious writings) depicted him as a black man with kinky hair, a wide nose, and thick lips (opposite of the fat bald guy you usually see). I had to check my emotions. I was like, wait a minute, you telling me Jesus and Buddha were black!

YouTube "Chinese's Ancestors were Africans" &

"SAMBO The Black God & Africans in Asia"

But, I found that the biggest hidden truth of them all is that African spirituality is the heart of all religion. The religion we get now has been boiled down to back fat; made fantasy by politicians of the old and new age and used to control the masses. The crazy part is that the same white religious leaders that have been staples in whitewashing world religion, praise original black face Madonna and child and honor black saints. Because the truth is that the black man (including woman) is the worship of God and conception! We created it. Yes, no matter how hard they try to hide it, you are the beginning. They changed your name, depicted you with blond hair and blue eyes, and repeated the lie so much that most of your parents and grandparents told it to you, intimately, as if it were the truth.

And the thing is, when I first saw all these connections; especially within Christianity and African spiritual systems like black Egypt (Kemet), I would come across books where many white authors would denote anything African-centered as pagan (not of God). I had to realize that by them strategically using that word, these "scholarly" white propagandist and their system of demonizing black culture had initially scared me away from diving into the root of black religious systems outside of Christianity.

The biggest hurdle as a #YBA is learning your true history and using it as a tool to uncover African spirituality (the root of the world's religions). Recognize that is has been repackaged with white-face. In fact, a large segment of the bible, like the book of Psalms and the 10 commandments, were taken directly off the walls of Kemet. Ever wonder why you say Amen after every prayer—it's common among Christians, Jews, and Muslims; but it's also the African God Amen-RA. Author Gerald Massey was one of the most notable scholars to point out the unmistakable reflections of the ancient spirituality of Kemet in modern Christianity.

Read *Before Genesis* by Robert Bridges

(provides a broader understanding of religion, the matters of race, politics, and origins in world religion and how it's all linked)

First let me ask you a simple question. How many books are in the bible? Well, that would have to depend on which bible you grab! Why is that? Why are some books left out of some bibles and included in others? Could the books that were left out said something the person in power didn't want you to know? [Google the Dead Sea Scrolls].

It just amazes me how people try to create an image of God and manipulate others with it. God is the one Devine being reigning over everything; even the galaxies we cannot see nor imagine. So how can you let someone imagine an image of a Divine Creator so great; black or white, male or female? I'm not convinced that there is a Christian truth of God; nor a Jewish, nor an Islamic, nor a Hindu, etc. There only exists the complete truth of God. The same God that made the universe as boundless as it stands. The One in which no boundaries apply.

If we can all agree on that, then what has the "institution" of religion done so far? The answer: divide and conquer. It has taken a general principal and dissected it into little pieces and created quibbles over whether one or the other is used for good or bad. For example, let's take the nuns uniform (a habit) which consists of a tunic covered by a scapular and a veil. This is no different than the chador (long dress) and Hijab (veil) worn by Islamic women. Generally, when you see a nun you are taught to think that they are very devote and modest covering and respecting themselves in the eyes of the Lord. But when you see a Muslim woman, you think that she is oppressed by her culture and must feel miserably hot in that thing. Why is this?

Religious brainwashing may be the strongest level of controlling a man and the "government" (in terms of political control) has been able to perpetuate this for ages. Do you think that you have avoided this manipulation?

YouTube "Brother Kaba Kamene—Moore Spirit"

(Sums up world religion historically in 7 mins)

Knowledge and Control

"The most potent weapon in the hands of the oppressor is the mind of the oppressed."

—Steven Biko

Egypt is the home and originator of what we know as the modern form Christianity. The original trinity in Egypt equaled the mother, the father, and the son. The Greeks took that and translated it into their own understanding in their books. The conquering Romans turned this into the father, the son, and the Holy Ghost; as the woman was cut out (which is crazy because all human kind originate from the womb of the woman which was represented with the original ankh).

YouTube Documentary by BBC "Osiris & Christianity-The Christian Adaptation of...

(Watch this whole thing and you're gonna be like... "you got ta be shitin' me")

Let's break down Jesus' existence; the real Jesus AKA Yesua AKA Yahusuha. [Please Google each name to find its meaning and origin.] First of all, Jesus was not a Christian. You wouldn't believe how many people say that he was in error.

Christians are the followers of Jesus. Jesus himself is said to be a Jew; but for chronological purposes, he is a Hebrew. [Please Google the difference between the term Jew and Hebrew.] When you Googled Yahusuha and its meaning, you may have come across the Hebrew alphabet. Notice anything strange? The letter "J" doesn't exist in the Hebrew language.

So wait a minute. Jesus is a Hebrew but there is no "J" in the Hebrew language, ancient or modern. So how's Jesus his name? The answer: it's not his original name. So what else have you been lied to about? Jesus with a "J" didn't exist until the Council of Nicaea where men of political rule gave him the title Christ. [Google the first Council of Nicaea.]

Ok, so his name isn't what you thought it was; but they wouldn't lie about the story of Yesua's life or his image, right? Well, in the bible it is written that he had feet like burnished bronze [Google this color]. I don't know about you; but, my feet are the same color as my face and arms. So, if Jesus' feet were the same color bronze as I am,; then, why is his face depicted white in all the mainstream pictures? Hint: Michaelangelo's Sistine Chapel ceiling of 1512. This was one of the main depictions of Jesus as a white man with European features. Before this, nearly all depictions of Jesus were of a colored man; even those of baby Jesus with Mary (the original Black Madonna and Child).

So what about the story of Jesus? In the religion of Islam—in which there is a great belief and respect for Jesus; unlike what is portrayed in the media—it is believed that Jesus didn't die; but ascended to the heavens to be with God and will return and some sects of Christianity believe the same thing. My point is, there exists so much more to the story than what's being told to you.

Read *The Book Your Church Doesn't Want You to Read*
Editor Tim Leedom (Pay special attention to the sub-chapter
"The World's Sixteen Crucified Saviors"

Google the following individuals; and write down a couple of
things about their life that are interesting to you:

Zoroaster:

_____
_____
_____

Osiris:

_____
_____
_____

Mithra (Mitra):

_____
_____

Buddha Sakia:

_____
_____
_____

Beddru of Japan:

_____
_____
_____

What exactly are your thoughts on these individuals,
their God-inspired purpose; and, the similarities and differences
amongst them all?

YouTube "The Darker Side of India" (It's pretty long but makes an awe-striking point)

Once you realize that the "institution of religion"—just as politics—is created to separate and oppress people, you gain a deeper perspective. The Romans persecuted Christians for years (3 centuries). They didn't just have a change of heart; but had a change in power and mindset. They used Christianity and the church to develop a power and control mechanism. When you begin to study the other major religions, you'll see that Christianity isn't the only religion used to ostracize and control people.

In the India documentary, you can see that the Dravidians (darker skinned Indian people) are treated worse than blacks in America. The lighter skinned Indians use religious scripture as a means of taking advantage and degrading darker Indians. They perpetuate this caste system in their school system, the job market, and in their society, at large.

These were exactly some of the practices "Christians" used in America to deprive African-Americans during slavery and civil rights. The KKK were nothing more than extremist Christians warping scripture to fit their alternative motive in discriminating based on race. Yet the media will quickly refer to the extreme Muslim as a terrorist. But for some reason, Christian extremists don't fit the bill to be called as they are.

What are your thoughts on how people use religion to justify the depression and degradation of other people?

_____

_____

_____

_____

Read *Make a Negro Christian* by Rev. Charles Colcock-Jones

(The original printing may be scarce, but you can find a reprinting with analysis.)

Christianity was taught to us in a manner of control; so a lot of universal truth in the religion was silenced and replaced with rules and traditions to keep the masses in line. This was as true for the early Christians under Roman control as it was for blacks under the rule of slavery. For instance, Nat Turner was a literate biblical scholar and preacher to his fellow slaves. Through his reading, fasting, and prayer he received word from God that it was time to fight the "Serpent;" it was time for the last to be first.

On August 22, 1831, he moved on this spiritual notion. He and his slave brigade killed about 60 white men, women, and children; freeing their slaves along the way. In retaliation, local militia and artilleries were gathered to kill over 200 blacks (even those whom had nothing to do with Turner).

The result of all of this was the Virginia General Assembly legislating law to make it illegal for slave to read and write also to restrict all blacks from holding religious meetings without the presence of a white minister. (Ever wonder why every black church you know has bible study on a Wednesday?) These laws spread all throughout the South.

YouTube "Prof James Small the facts about Vodun AKA Voodoo"

(What they don't tell you about the African spiritual system in school)

Understand that I'm not writing this to shake your faith. In fact, I hope that a greater exposure to a little truth will be refreshing and will greatly increase your faith in a Universal God (the one all human kind and space originate from); while exposing the manipulation that truth and spirituality has undergone due to man's non-understanding and addiction to obtaining power and control over others. Personally, this has truly opened my eyes up to the crookedness of people in pursuit of money, power, and the false reverence they accomplish through their use of inflicting fear onto others.

Now maybe after reading this section some of you may be so grounded in the "common era" (which I refer to as "common errors") knowledge that's been passed down to you that you either dispel everything you just read; **or, it sparked some thought that was in the deep crevasse of your mind** and now you have so many other questions—**that's called creative thinking or revolution**. Let's write down all that brain activity before it gets clouded:

_____

_____

_____

_____

_____

_____

_____

_____

_____

I'm not trying to lead you anywhere in particular (as far as religion or conversion goes). I just want you to think, "Why is this truth purposely hidden?"

Now, will you or I ever know the complete truth? Probably not! But I feel like each lie uncovered pleases the Creator. Like most believe that cleanliness is next to Godliness, I believe that the truth is the closest thing to the true Universal Creator. I'm not convinced that there is a Christian truth of God; nor a Jewish, nor an Islamic, nor a Hindu, etc. There only exists the universal truth of God.

I don't practice a distinctive "religion," but I am continually committed to cultivating a rounded spirituality—which I reference as a Creationist (not to be confused with the conventional Creationism)—under my own terms; where ancient religious texts and scientific explanation are juxtaposed. I believe in one powerful concentration of intelligence that is the Begetter of everything in this world; our galaxy and the next, and whatever else is out there.

Whether this Omnipresent Intelligence is of a male or female energy, I don't know. But I am forever grateful for its mercy. I believe that this universal intelligence has been translated through many prophets (Osiris, Buddha, Yahosua AKA Jesus, Zorastor, Muhammad, **and the many women that have been silenced by "his-story,"** etc.). It becomes clearer that science in its pure exploratory state, proves God's presence; and the unknown rests on faith. For everything of the Creator doesn't have to be laid out for mere human understanding. Imagine what havoc we would wreak if we did know of these wonders!

The Christian Jig-A-Boo: "Welcome to the show ladies and gentlemen"

YouTube "Jig-A-Boo" A poem by Jackie Hill

In the 50s and 60s, the church used to be the cornerstone of our community. This is no longer the reality. There is a huge disconnect between our youth today and organized religion. Maybe it's because of the hypocrisy or the lack of substantiated knowledge and growth? These were the very reasons I myself experienced a brief stall in interaction with the "church." I found a greater sense of truth and knowledge through personal spiritual search and investigation. To be clear, I do encourage a gathering of like-minds; and I definitely see the need in the encouragement that the gathering provides. But when people "play" church, it all becomes null and void.

Many of our churches have been overrun by the "stunnas" addressed earlier in Chapter 1. Easter Sunday becomes the fashion show of the year—when half of the people in the church make their 1st and last appearance in their best dressed. 1st Sundays are always full of collection plate plugs. Christmas service turns into a ticket frenzy and a competition between which church can pack the most seats. Nowadays, Pastors feel entitled to private jets. Creflo Dollar was a fool for that one. The "building fund" has become the means for the modern age erecting of the Tower of Babel; with double wide flat screens (with prompts telling you to check-in via your fave social media app) and a speaker system designed to deafen God.

And my only question is, "Is it all really serving its purpose?"

I know that there still exists those grassroots community-based black churches. But on the larger scale of things, church has become big business. It's so resource-based that you can only really get the type of help you need in a middle class area; where the preacher will check with the financial department to make sure you're up on your tithes before you can "qualify" for aid this quarter. Now, I don't know just how this problem can be fixed; but if this section struck a chord with you, please voice your opinion and/or solution.

Chapter Notes:

_____

_____

_____

_____

_____

_____

_____

_____

_____

_____

_____

_____

_____

_____

_____

_____

_____

_____

Chapter 5: On My Erykah Badu and Lauryn Hill Shit

Soundtrack for this chapter *Mama's Gun* **by Erykah Badu &** *MTV Unplugged No. 2* **by Lauryn Hill** (Yes the entire albums!)

Now that the deprograming has begun, it's time to figure out who YOU are; and who you plan on being. It's time to take control of your own life. Enlightenment is near. Dropping the shackles and coming into the act of being is a journey in itself. This means, defining your own labels and establishing a positive self-image; ultimately coming into consciousness.

Understanding **your** supreme connection with the Creator of the universe and all of the natural things within the universe equates to harmony and achieving a certain level of spiritual ascension. The physiological state of the mind is stronger than the physical over-powering of a slave driver. You have to understand what true freedom is; you must want to be free; and, you must **act** on that desire (moving in a direction that will likely be contrary to society).

Understanding How Powerful You Are

You have to understand how important it is to make and shape your own perception of yourself. If you don't, another person will! They will tell you what to think of yourself and define your capabilities. If you don't open your eyes wider to the world and internally to your true self, you will revert back to insecurities (those perpetrated in society, at large). This is what "the system" has been able to do by cutting you off from your pre-slavery history. Right now, your perception of yourself may be small; and that's fine! It's what you do from this moment on to widen that perception.

What is your current (honest) perception of yourself? (Use exact and descriptive words.)

_____

_____

_____

_____

_____

_____

_____

Bonus Track "My Uzi" by David Banner ft. Big K.I.R.T.

_____

I think that the 1st thing you should realize is how connected you are to the world around us; and the universe at large. But what the hell does that really mean right? I don't just mean that in the emotional or spiritual sense of "I am the world," but also, in a literal sense.

Every second that you breathe, you are breathing oxygen from plants that take the carbon dioxide you expel to create more oxygen. With as many people and animals on this earth and as many times as this process occurs (a million gazillion times), how many gulps of air do you think that you have "shared" with someone else? Literally a breath went completely through someone else's body, got recycled by a plant, and entered your body, then a plant again, and through somebody else's body or an animal.

Even crazier than that, imagine the millions/billions of (ancient) people who have died (mind you civilization is over 14 million years old), been buried, and decayed into "plant food"; and helped in this never ending process. I'm pretty sure you have breathed an atom or two that has existed for hundreds of thousands; if not a couple of million years before you were even thought about. More impressive than breathing the same breath as someone, is the fact that the very atoms that you are made of are literally billions of years old.

Brian Clegg in his book, *The Universe Inside You*, further explains how hydrogen, helium, and lithium from the Big Bang theory formed matter—the very same organic molecules in your body; and the same elements of stardust. So literally and metaphysically speaking, YOU ARE A STAR—no bullshit! I never learned that in my science class☹. Had I known the true connection I have to space, Science classes would have been a bit more interesting. [YouTube "Young Pharaoh Allah: The Melanated Body Aquarian Ascension" (start at mark 13:50)]

You should see the true connection to everything; from the sky, to the grass, to your very existence. But, it's harder to fully grasp the idea of nature because most of us live in "concert jungles" (inner-cities full of infrastructure and buildings) where we don't have a true conception and understanding of the workings of nature.

We generally waste so much time crooning over celebrities and other "popular" people that we never learn to appreciate how special we are, individually. You have an exponential amount of atoms in your body (7×10^{27}) that were once atoms in space and you're special enough to have your own fingerprint (not replicated by any other human)! Out of the gazillion people that have lived; or will live, not one of them have your same fingerprint... I'mma let that sync in. Now, my question to you is, how in the world will you make your print mean something?

Step one in that process requires you to maintain the best **you** at all times. A humbling part of doing this is learning to take better care of yourself on a physical, mental, and spiritual level:

- **Physical:** You have to fully understand that your body is, a well-structured collection of minerals (the very same as the Earth). You must respect nature and your body; as it's the source of all; even your electronics are composed of mineral (Earthy) elements (i.e. alkaline batteries). Learn how the body interacts with healing herbs and crystals. One of the ways you can evaluate your body's balance is by checking your poop as a sign of health. [Google image of the chart "How Well Do You Know Your Shit?"] You are made up of about 70-80% water, which holds more memory than any organic element. Your body has a continual need for vitamins, detoxing, water (Alkaline vs. "purified" water), and exercise. The fast food and junk food you continue to eat is full of stuff that slows you down and doesn't necessarily keep you going at your optimum level. Look into fasting as an act of both detoxing the body and clearing the mind. Hopefully you kind of have a slightly deeper recognition of who you really are and what you are made of, literally. You hear the clichés "being one with nature" and "ashes to ashes, dust to dust." You must literally look at what your body needs to survive and realize that you are the same as the Earth, in a sense.

- **Mental:** You have to fully understand the power and influence your mental state has on your physical state. The need for counseling, expression, relaxing, and relieving stress (which can complicate health issues if not dealt with properly) are all necessities in maintaining mental health. There have probably been some semi-dramatic occurrences you've experienced. They can manifest if you don't deal with them. Stresses (family, school, work, and being black in America) can take a toll. All the strategic noise of society blocks us in achieving mental serenity/peace. Through consistent mediation and prayer practices, along with prioritizing things that are important to you, you can reach that peace.

- **Spiritual**: You have to fully understand the eternal character of your soul. You are not only a compilation of those minerals and vitamins; but, you hold a soul. Understanding (especially after the religion breakdown) that no one organization should; or can, regulate your individual spirituality is the main key. It's yours and should remain a personal thing of which you don't necessarily have to categorize yourself. You have a great responsibility compared to everything else in nature. Spiritual wellness evolves through reading thought provoking material, understanding who you are as a black person, gathering with like minds to encourage growth, and maintaining a grounded mental state (via prayer and meditation).

Further along your journey you will begin to realize that all 3 of these things are interconnected; and if you don't keep them in balance, then problems can persist. There is a certain balance we as humans need to keep with nature physically, mentally, and spiritually.

> **Personal Reflection:** My junior year in high school, Erykah Badu came to Lincoln for a speaking event. She brought the D.O.C (featured in the NWA movie *Straight Outta Compton*) and a couple of other folks. In this packed auditorium of teenagers—after a deep convo about rap—she began to talk about chakras in the body and the focusing of energy and … blah, blah, blah. We had no idea what she was talking about (especially since our science classes hadn't exposed us to the truth that we all have magnetic forces in our bodies—reasoning behind sliding across the floor and shocking

somebody). I tried to really listen (even though I didn't fully understand). I only got pieces of information because she spent ½ the time telling us to be quiet. I didn't realize what she was trying to share, then. Ironically enough, ten years later, I have begun to comprehend and use that same information to better understand myself and use this energy. With that being said, I do understand how all of this information may feel—overwhelming and a bit confusing. Honestly, it may take you a couple of years to "react" to most of the things explored in this book. My main objective, however, is to give you a little glimpse of light so that when it hits you 5 to 10 years from now, you can just smile and better contemplate your next steps.

Falling into the Background

Mouth wide-shut, fingers tucked (inside my pockets).

Thoughts firing off like rockets, but I continue to slide back—back into the background, too scared to make a sound. Don't wanna sound stupid, draw attention to my difference. Shouldn't be different. I just wanna be like everybody else; rather that than being myself.

If I look like, dress like, talk like... then it'll be alright. Yeah that's easier.

Background Music

Heard that Mike Brown dude got shot-down down the street in a neighborhood like mine, in attire that kinda resemble mine, had a stature that kinda match mine. I would stand up and say something about it, but it ain't my business, nor my concern. I'll just fall back, back into this background, let this beat ride and watch out a little better to guard my own back

Background Music

I really don't feel comfortable in these heels, and my tiddies feel like they bout to fall out of this shirt, but it'll look real cute when I start to twerk. Told Keshia I didn't wanna go to this club, but I gotta ride cuz she my girl. Just as long as I don't get as drunk as last time. I mean, damn I didn't mean to sleep with him, he blew up my timeline and threatened to show the snapchat vid, then told all his boys I wasn't shit, posted pics of me on Facebook... it's cool tho, next week it'll be some other chick; as long as I'm the baddest in the club tonight, it'll be alright—hope we don't get into a fight.

Background Music

Stood out on the block long enough last night. Had to re-up twice, but made enough to get right—New J's on deck. Gotta hit up school tomorrow; aint been in a few weeks, but I gotta show 'em my shoe game on fleek. Just hope I don't come on a test week, aint trying to be no real student. The way the system set up now, I ain't gotta do no real work no-how: just show up for that attendance check and graduation on deck. Ain't got time for that college thang, this cash on the street too easy to claim.

Background Music

Note to Reader:

Who are you to be simple? A part of the crowd, bland, recused? For you are down playing every bit of what makes you unique, special, and an individual.

You play that low level beat in the background, but you're meant to be those bold vocals in the foreground. Recite your flow on top of that beat; flip that chorus and blow the speakers. For the meek are without presence... Just ask Meek Mills (pun intended).

AGAINST THE GRAIN:

There exists, my friend, a need to change,

A need to open one's mind beyond the bounds of societal limitations.

Limitations purposely constructed—setting the frame of your mindset, build imaginary walls to constrict your thought, like a mime trapped in that boundless box–an oxymoron on its face.

But let's face it, that's how most of our race runs this race— can't shoot a hoop, jump that hurdle then you stuck forever in that mottled pool of mediocrity

A nobody, because they tricked you into thinking you were less than what God made you.

But there exists in all of us, a piece of God,

A piece of innovation that has to shine beyond the crushing confines of which we allow other brainwashed people to place upon us this voluntary choke-hold.

These limitations are upheld with an iron fist—systematic "failures" which serve their purpose:

In all truth, we know the rich profit off of poverty, the selling of poor education that yields a working-poor, confused by their lack of acceleration and the heavy chain of student loans and debt, yet and still force fed education is the key.

There exists, in a few, a fearless desire and mission to go against the grain.

To acquire a higher sense of self—connecting to a deeper sense of wealth in truth.

But truth, my friend has become a fraudulent commodity—bought, watered-down, sold on a market based not in actuals; but greed and the appeal of its packaging.

Internal truth has been clouded with material gain. The masses have been so fooled that the presentation of truth cannot penetrate; it's shunned and quickly marked "crazy"; and then assassinated systematically–Martin, Malcolm, Medgar, YOU and your potential!... Against the grain.

Slave Education in the 21st Century

YouTube "F**k I Look Like" A poem by Kai Davis

How many of you ever found yourself bored at school? Maybe it's because the public school system isn't setup to serve you; but for you to serve it. What do I mean by that? On a daily basis, #YBAs are herded like cattle into special ED classes, undergo numerous state sponsored tests to hold them back from graduation, and are held captive in outdated mold infested facilities. Who benefits from keeping these conditions so ratchet? City and state government—racking in thousands of dollars for sustaining the status quo. A lot of times, this money is funneled to higher preforming districts—rich white ones.

In addition to making money for keeping you educationally suppressed, the system wins on both ends because the subpar information passed down to you throughout your "educational journey" is lack luster; to say the least. #YBAs, on average, graduate from high school with lower levels of reading, math, and science comprehension; partially as a result of the conditions of the school districts they come from. Some kids are then intimidated by higher education; or, just plainly have no interest in it because of the manner in which education has been administered to them. There is a disconnect between #YBA's lives, experiences, and innate African centered understanding. [For a more complete breakdown of this concept please YouTube "Booker T. Colman Educating our youth for the 21st century." He breaks down a student's individual learning preference and how the current system isn't catering to these learning preferences.]

True knowledge empowers you and gives you the ability to operate independently; not cripple you, your frame of mind, and trap you in a box. I truly believe that the public education system's political agenda is to keep the poor, poor. An obvious example is the fact that public schools don't TEACH FINANCIAL LITERACY! Right now, the largest growing section of indebted people are those collecting student loan debt.

Booker T. Coleman (known as Kaba Kamene), a retired Board of Education Director and professor, has extensively explored the broken public system; and has pinpointed exactly why our current system doesn't serve the purpose of educating and liberating black kids, in particular. Basically, the European curriculum is limited and very fragmented in structure. His key point is that the European model teaches a broken and unconnected segment of knowledge that doesn't completely allow the African-American child to connect the dots across multiple disciplines—as we are holistic learners.

The European curriculum model is nothing like the original African-centered style of learning; of which, the European acquired much if not all of its knowledge from (minus the misconceptions and manipulations they later cultivated). The misconceptions and manipulations arose during the conquering of African people and knowledge. The procession generally flows: Greeks admired and learned from the Africans, the Greeks manipulated knowledge to fit their culture and make the knowledge inclusive of themselves, the Romans stole the knowledge (including actual written books) from the Greeks and certain areas of Africa (Egypt being the most evident place of seizure). From that point on, everything got mottled, misinterpreted and redistributed on a large scale.

Sound Track: Strange Fruition by Lupe Fiasco

The objective here is to not get tricked out of your own history. Let's talk about what you know (or should I say what you think you know). All of what you think you know is likely ½ truths. I personally think that we; especially in the African American community, are still victims of the "slave education" system. We all know during slavery up until about the Jim Crow era, black folks were legally denied access to education. You couldn't pick up a book or even read the bible. White preachers (many of whom couldn't read themselves) told your ancestors what they wanted them to hear.

One of the most famous lines used to shape a slaves religious mindset was that it was written in God's book that a slave should toil in this world (to work like a dog); and collect their riches in heaven. Meaning if you are a "good" slave on earth, the Lord will reward you upon your death. This insinuated that death was the only exit from slavery. That pretty much doesn't fly these days. But sadly, that same slave education is being circulated still today because even though they allow us read, they are still practicing ramped censorship, cultivating lies, and rewriting our history and selling it to us as a "textbook."

The most hilarious, yet insulting, attempt of this has occurred in Texas. A well-known public school text publisher (McGraw-Hill) has revised its history books to narrate that the U.S. system of slavery as an internship where "workers" brought over to America (in terms of immigration) and were taught agriculture. The largest pile of bullshit I've heard in a while!

Minimalizing the slave trade and its impact on America greatly slights the African American dysfunction syndrome we're experiencing now. It eases white guilt! Without our complete history, it kind of looks like black people are just screwed up for no reason; and mainly because white America doesn't want a finger pointing back at them. They do it to other minorities too, just as they have done with rewriting the history on how America gained much of what was once Mexico so as to not incite rebellion amongst the large population of young Hispanics in the South. Let's not forget the concentration camps the government forced the Japanese into here on American soil in the 40s. They just want to gloss over all that shit.

By starting out black history at slavery, the entire educational system cuts off our identity; and our deep connection to principles that our ancestors cultivated throughout the world. Recognize that a system that teaches you to understand vs. "over-stand" is enforcing a limitation upon you. If I teach you just what/how much I want you to know and not the infinite truth, do I not possess the power to control you and what you think? Am I not stifling your growth? Why isn't the education system catering to exactly who you are; and what you will need to know by the time you graduate?

Giving white people the authority to rewrite our history, without thorough investigation, has paralyzed our ability to define who we are and pin down our true origins. Our history has been whitewashed; but all we have to do to take it back is READ! As a #YBA you should start your independent study under people who look like you. Once you start this, you will begin to connect a lot of the ½ truths to reality. A lot of concepts will finally begin to make sense.

YouTube "Why do blacks still feel like N-GGAZ in the 21st century? Frances C Welsing"

We have to remember that just like white people created the current perception of black people through over exaggerated depictions in media; so too have they created the great white hype in the very same way. So much media is pushed out with white people as the leaders, kings, Adams and Eves that we think that our presence in history isn't as iconic or ancient as theirs. [Please Google the Dogon people of Africa.]

I remember going into my local library one summer. I was picking up random books in the geography section. I picked up one well illustrated book about migration or something. I just so happened to turn the page to North America and saw that archeologist found artifacts that dated cultural market trades between American Indians and Africans via westward migrations of Africans BEFORE SLAVERY AND BEFORE COLUMBUS! Meaning Africans made their way to America on ships that they built themselves; and traded with Indian people well before the white man even knew "America" existed.

Because of white media propaganda, you #YBAs think of Africa as some extended Feed the Children commercial. Let me tell you that it's everything but! Africa literally is the richest continent in the world; culturally and wealth-wise. (I'm not talking about that worthless paper note you carry in your wallet.) Gold, diamonds, oil, you name it; and the African Earth provides it. Why do you think that it was the chosen birth place of man?

Some of the well-traveled and best educated people I know are from Africa. During my undergrad years, the Africans I met on campus had been to private boarding schools, had personal drivers back home, and spent their summers in London. I was like, "What the heck am I missing here?"

The cockiest (in a good way) of all the Africans I knew seemed to be the Nigerians. (There goes that word again NGR, NiGeRians.) They are true Nigeritos; and they know it! I think that's where their confidence radiated from. We here in America need to revert back to that same self-knowledge.

Anyway, Africa is the Mecca; past and present. They got you thinking black people are running around in dirt huts. Africa is the birth place of the modern day mansion (i.e. castles). There are castles all over Africa; even ruins that predate English castle work by hundreds of years. Who the heck do you think taught the white man to build them? Answer: a real Negrito. Moors in early Europe ended the Dark Ages around 711 A.D. bringing about the Renaissance era.

Know that everything has a cause and an effect. Ever wonder why they didn't ever really tell you the cause of the Renaissance? [Google the conditions of Europe before Moorish intervention (the Dark Ages).] I mean it wasn't like white people in Europe just woke up and started reading and writing. Moors from Africa saved the European from the invading Germanic tribes; and then, proceeded to help them restructure their society by building schools, teaching whites how to read Arabic, introducing edible spices and eating utensils, music, clothes, soap, and building castles and structures with streetlights (basically domesticating them). [To learn more about this read *The African Presence in Early Europe* by Ivan van Sertima.]

Random Thought: Google the black kings of Hawaii

(Just in case you didn't know that such a thing even existed)

In fact, Europe's fascination with America came from the African's (Moors) that conquered Europe during its dark ages. Columbus wouldn't have even made it to South America without the direction of skilled black seamen; as Moors knew how to travel via celestial patterns. Now, I'm going to ask you another simple question. By now, you should know that the answer is probably not that simple. What's today's date? You probably won't find the answer on your phone or your computer screen. That's because true time is written in the sky. You see, the school system didn't even teach you how to properly tell time! You should know the 1st calendar was found in Africa (Nabta Playa) dating back beyond 6500 years ago. The white man changed the calendar. [Google the difference in A.D., B.C, and B.C.E.]

YouTube "Eddie Griffin: Slavery, Spirit, the Black Woman, and More"

Coming into consciousness is a scary thing because you begin to "see" not just with your eyes; but with your mind. The ability to "over-stand" vs understand what's really going on and how things and symbols are interrelated down to the smallest detail is crucial in recognizing what will lead to true ascension, or, to your ultimate demise.

Flip It

What if God looked like anything other than a white man?

What if Jesus real name was Yeshua; and he was a colored man?

What if the last was really the first?

What if a black woman birthed the world's population?

What if the minority was the majority?

What if the hood resided in the suburbs?

What if politicians told the unadulterated truth?

What if we spent more on education & world hunger, than war?

What if cops weren't so quick to shoot first & frame the scene second?

What if you knew that #blacklivesmatter?

What if Columbus really discovered America?

What if America was really the land of the free?

What if millions of Americans were really killed by foreign "terrorist" on 911?

What if politicians really cared about our soldiers sent to die over $, oil, & bragging rights?

What if humans displayed some sense of humanity towards one another?

Some of us are so grounded in falsehoods.

What's real to you? Truth. *Hopeful wishes*. Or **lies.**

YouTube Documentary "911 Loose Change" and "Ferinheight 911"

Caution:

P.C. (political correctness) Check

To white people that may be reading this next section aloud; especially along with black people, you might want to let a black person read exclusively, or take a vote on whether or not all the black people in the room are ok with you saying the actual N-word.

I'm O.N. (Original Nigga)

Hello my dear comrade,

Hi my friend,

Hey buddy,

WHAT'S UP MY NIGGA!

See, I'd rather be yo nigga, cuz we be familiar. We be the same; something like looking through a mirror—you know, share the same pain. We move through life on the same wave.

We, we be kin; bound by the same skin—melinated deep as a mahogany seated mandolin. Strummin' on its strings, we speak the same voice—ebonics just so happens to be our method of choice.

Sounds as sweet as yo Granny's grin—more Southern than that old school bathtub gin. Deeper than cotton-seeded fields bassin' with soulful Negro-spirituals, cuz see our people, we be so lyrical…

　　　　-or at least we use to be

Use to know our own worth, but now-a-dayz niggas seem to need a spiritual re-birth.

Use to know we gave nativity to the earth via a **black** virgin birth,

Use to know that niggas roamed the lands and owned the sands,

Use to know that niggas navigated the seas before white people could even speak

　　　　-maybe I should slow-up cuz I really didn't mean to get that deep… BUT

We use to know that "NIGGA" was the calling of God manifesting itself unto itself, resonating upon the skies.

You see my niggas, real niggas knew, that the sun in the sky connected to the gleam in your eye—reflected the moon in the dark sky that projected the melanin into the atmosphere.

-or did you not even know that there was melanin in the atmosphere?

-We use to know

Real niggas knew that we had the largest connect with the celestial set, where our oldest niggas plotted the course of the stars over 6,500 years ago at Nabta Playa (in Africa).

-we use to know

Real niggas know that our people are so regal that the Ultimate Divine itself blessed their feet beneath—allowed them to walk on gold-plated tectonics and the diamond-crusted valleys of mother Africa.

-we use to know

Real niggas knew we were master teachers—that we civilized the European and gave influence to the Korean—we are the original people.

You see nigger [N-I-G-G-E-R] is just a misnomer by the white man that didn't completely understand the essence of a tru nigga, because before this,

We were NEGALs of Uruguay— meaning teachers.

And before that, we were NAGAS of India—meaning serpent gods.

And before that, we were NEGAS of Ethiopia—meaning Serpent King of kings.

And before that, we were NIGERS of Nigeria—meaning Emperors.

And before that, we were NEGGURS (NGR) of Egypt—GOD!

So the next time you see yo nigga on the street, and you solute yo nigga with a, "What's up my nigga!"... just make sure you remind that nigga what it really means to be an ORIGINAL NIGGA!

"My Nigga"

Quote: "follow no nigga, except the god in front of my mirror"

-Wale (the rapper)

Simeon called Niger (ACTS 13:1)

Now many older members of the black community despise the infamous "N-word." If you yourself are used to letting the word fly without regard, I'm sure you fix your mouth when you get around your grandmother, great-Aunt, the pastor, etc. But, let the setting be just right, you know that same pastor or grandmother would be ready to call somebody a nigga if the term so fit the person they were talking about.

Hilariously enough, Rev. Al Sharpton attempted to end the use of the "N-word" completely in July of 2007 by having a protest/funeral to "bury" the use of the word. They literally walked the street with a casket. My personal reaction was, "Are these niggas serious! (SMH ROTF)" Then, in July of 2008, Jesse Jackson got caught on air of a FOX interview with a hot mic on and called President Obama a nigga. That was classic, am I right?

You see older black people use it as a form of expression (usually negative). In our generation, we use it somewhat as a form of endearment. But, let someone outside of our community utter the word and it's an entirely different reaction. I have heard white people ask, "Well if it's so offensive if a white person says it, then why do they (black people) say it to each other; especially in rap music?"

I've even had to let some of the older white people in my work environment know that ultimately that's something that they will never understand, because it is not for them to understand. That just seems to be something white people will never fully accept. If they can't have it; then no one should, right? (A touch of white privilege.) Black people can, and often do, call each other the "N-word". Not simply because we can; but because there is a deeper connection to the word amongst ourselves. There exists a sense of connection to this word—pain, hurt, struggle, success, family, fight—that a white person can never understand in that very same sense.

When we say that word amongst ourselves, we have this unification between the person saying it or receiving it; as we've been through similar incidents based on our skin, our hardships, and our ancestral history. When a white person utters this word, it's an insult, PERIOD POINT BLANK. (Because 9 out of 10 times someone in their lineage had a part in the cause of said pain, hardship, and hurtful history.)

Nigger is a fighting word simply because white people have no connection to the pain, the hurt, the struggle, the success, the family, or the fight that the word is drenched in—the black experience. A white person's use of the word is connected to the slave-master, to the oppressor and they can only use it as a way to further hurt a black person because that is the **only** connotation the word has had within their use of it.

A white person's disconnect is more so evident in the fact that about 80 to 90% of them will pronounce "NIGG-ER" and not nigga—expressing a superiority distinction; and not a commonality between sender and receiver. That slave-master rhetoric is loud and clear. Let me be loud and clear in the fact that even if a white person pronounces "nigga," it's still a fighting word.

Furthermore, my question to any white person who would ask the question of why black people can use the word when a white person cannot is, "Why in the hell would you (as a white person) want to call a black person a nigger or a nigga in the first place?" The only thing a black person would think is that you're degrading them—even in this hip hop era.

This brings me to my next point. We, as black people, sometimes can give too much of our own power away; especially when it comes to that word. I'm not saying that we shouldn't get angry when the word is used as a derogatory epithet. What I am suggesting is that a much needed cultural shift take place within the black community.

That cultural shift is the realization that the "N-word" is much more than the rot-images of slavery and the stout connotation of bigotry. For so long, we have taken on white superiority views. We constantly define things in the manner in which the white superiority complex would. We have allowed them to define and dictate our histories; and consequently, that will further allow them to dictate our future to a certain extent.

My case lies in the derivative of the word NIGGER. Because of the European and Spanish slave masters, we associate this word in a negative manner. We have allowed them to carve out what a nigger is, when in fact, they (the white man) had no idea how to pronounce the word or its true origins. But like black folk—stripped of our language, heritage, and common African sense—we went along with the lie, bought into the "nigger syndrome" and tried everything in our power not to be seen as a nigger in the eyes of the white man.

Let's get a little history on the word to bring a little context to the conversation. The word is older than Jesus, no lie. Our history as black people and that word goes deeper than most of the scared religious writings of the world. Right now, you're probably reading this with a distorted face trying veraciously to reconcile some kind of meaning or comprehension in what I just said.

First of all, Nigger (in some form or another) was used in other regions aside from America's reference of slavery. So many times, we as black people allow the views of how the white American man portrays us in slavery that we have lost our sense of self; as we have to break the connection of the word from the American white man. For starters, let's go to the bible, specifically; the King James Version.

> Now there were at Antioch, in the church that
> was there, prophets and teacher, Barnabas, and
> Symeon that was called Niger, and Lucius of
> Cyrene, and Manaen the foster-brother of
> Herod the tetrarch, and Saul.

-ACTS 13:1

Symeon, a "niger" (with only one 'g'), was a prophet or a teacher. I would assume "niger" was used to denote his color; but anyone that has researched the bible's characters and the geography of the locations would know that majority of the people in the bible were of color (despite how they choose to cast or depict them in movies and books).

So, why would they reserve this as a descriptor for just one person of color in the whole bible? How many pastors or priest do you know that will repeat the phrase exactly as they read? You see that the lists of people were denoted as prophets and teachers; one of the earlier derivate of the N-word was Nagel; which meant teacher

The King James Version, one of the 1st English translations, was finished in 1611 A.D. and we were "nigers" then. So maybe we should start there. Is a "nigger" by any other name still a "niger"?

When researching the etymology of the word or the variations of it, you may find a couple interesting things: 1) Niger is a country in West Africa [north of Nigeria—which also contains the word]. 2) Niger is also the name of a river in Africa that flows into the Gulf of Guinea. 3) The word has several variations. "Neger" and "Negar" derive from the Spanish and Portuguese word Negro; "Ne`gre" derives from French.

Largely, you will find that the etymological origin for the word is accredited to Latin—Niger, meaning black. The problem with this, according to authors Shaba Shabaka and Dr. Ernie A. Smith (Professor of Clinical Linguistics), is that the root word of which the Latin language derives Niger from is inconclusively founded. Meaning that the word does not truly originate from Latin; and no one knows how the word was introduced to that language.

Shabaka and Smith detail in their book, Nigger *a Divine Origin,* how this fact alone is a tale-tale sign that the Latin language borrowed this word from another language. The two authors further point out that "NGR" the **written** root of the word of "niger" pre-dates to at least 4000 B.C.E. in Africa (Egypt) and has also appeared in other civilizations such as Babylon and Punt. NGR is found in the root word of the names of the God that gave birth to humanity (a female goddess named **Neggur**) in regions like Ethiopia, Kemet, Nubia (Sudan), and India. Shabaka contends that these people refereed to themselves as the people of God, **NiGR**itic people. Variations of these people were the Nagran people of Ethiopia (black people), the Ngirri people of Babylon (black people), and the Naga people of India (black people). We referred to ourselves as such before the white man came in, mispronounced, and bastardized our God given name.

See our **Neggur**—known as the God of all gods—was so fresh that they had to copy her story of creating man from clay off the walls of Kemet into the text of the Bible [YouTube: The Immortal Cells of Henrietta Lacks].

Soundtrack "New Slave" by Kanye West

With Hip Hop today, the commercialization of the word has totally denigrated its divinity; mostly because they have put it up for sell. [Please read Appendix D.] The industry has taken this word and our culture and used it to make money. If you really listen to Kanye's lyrics, you see that the type of money we're dealing with isn't just from a record sale. White industry leaders control the tempo of music content out here. (Ask Plies—a rapper who was told that he had to take a record off of his album because he used the word "cracker" once; but all his nigga-songs were cleared for release.) [YouTube "Plies talks Trayvon Martin, 'Cracker' vs The N-Word & Lawsuit.]

The people that own the "industry" of hip hop continue to sale us "niggas" and "keys" (kilos). This illusion reverberates, when the real truth about heavy drug abuse equates to white boys and prescription drugs. I mean really, when was the last time you saw a crackhead? And a young one at that?

I personally haven't seen a crackhead under the age of 35-40, only the antique ones over 50 or so. What you see on a regular basis are functioning pill poppers, young and old, white and black (and brown and yellow for that matter). Honestly, I see more young white meth-heads in their teens and twenties. But this dysfunction doesn't seem to be as marketable as niggas and kingpin street dealers. Why is this?

The white corporate owners and distributors of the music industry have legitimately been linked, on paper, to owning large stock in privatized prisons. They then make millions off of artists (especially those that sign bad deals) in the hip hop business that use the word "nigga." These artists rap about an exaggerated lifestyle that most have never even lived—which include grave criminal acts. The impressionable listeners of such music buy into this lifestyle illusion and easily become participants who ultimately end up serving time at the "university" making for-profit end items during their sentence, when said stockholders repeatedly double and triple their income. It's all a game to them.

Well I'm here to let you know that my "nigga" ain't cheap! I'm proud of my "nigga." I fully respect my "nigga." And I won't be ran by their "nigger."

YouTube "You gone get this work" poem by Jasmine Mans

We need to get back to the real. That word means community to us. We own it when we respect it; however that respect may look. At the White House Correspondence dinner, Obama put that swag on his last appearance and left in true playa fashion with his last remark being, "Obama out (literal mic drop)" complete with the side glance while he walked away… I know at least half of the black people watching this from home said to themselves, "That's my nigga." Well to top it off, the comedic host Larry Wilmore, a black man, took the words right out of our mouths and said them out loud. "Yo, Barry... You did it my nigga." All the white people had a silent heart attack, I'm sure.

But we know what was up. That was that connection.

YouTube "Konscious Konnect- Sypher PT2

Un-plagiarized "Roots:" Connecting My Own Dots

YouTube Sunni Patterson "We Made It" Def Jam Poetry

One day at work, during the Ferguson riots, a white co-worker and I begin talking on the subject matter because it was the #1 trending topic on the front page of Yahoo. She focused on the idea that it was crazy what these people were doing to their own neighborhood (burning and looting). My 1st point was that the media was focusing more on that in order to draw away from the case. My 2nd point to her was if you're a people that has no way else to make your plight be heard, then what else do you have to make your point with?

When you treat a people unjustly history just continues to repeat itself (i.e. the riots of Chicago and LA). When you start burning shit, people finally start to listen and it's mostly because they don't want it in the papers and across the internet where other countries begin to realize how bad your race relations are.

As we were having this conversation another coworker (white) walked up and caught the middle of our conversation. I began to talk and started with, "My people..." As the second coworker cut me off and said, "Aren't I your people? We're all American." I continued to correct her. I told her, "I'm black before I'm anything!" (And that was what I meant by my people.)

I could tell that kind of threw her off. But she continued to say that she teaches her granddaughter that we're all American; even though her skin is a little more brown than hers. Her granddaughter is mixed with Polynesian or something. I told her that's great; but, her granddaughter should know and recognize her difference and celebrate her Polynesian culture (in order to fully understand who she is). My coworker looked at me crazy because all she thought was important was the American.

We, as black people, can't fall for that! At all times, we have to know that we are black. We need to know what that really means as a whole; and individually. This means we must fully reacquaint ourselves with our ancestors.

The thought of actually tracing back to that one original ancestor to come over on the boat is a completion that I would love to accomplish; and that is really important in completely relating to who we are. In Africa, understanding lineage and paying tribute to one's ancestors is a very big deal. I set out to get as close as possible to doing this by retracing my maternal side (especially since I fall into that "I got a deadbeat—biological—daddy" category).

I remember going over my great-great grandmother's house all the time. My family is young—meaning almost everybody had their kids early—so she was around her mid 80's at the time I remember her most. My older cousin would tell me stories about our great-great aunts and the male progenitor of our family (a white man with a red mustache); and how he was rumored to have owned a plantation.

My cousin would also tell me stories about how my great-great grandmother would have to persistently turn down white men that approached her because they didn't know that she was black. She didn't want to create any confusion; especially in that time in the South. While I would sit up in the bed and listen to these sound bites of history, somebody would always throw in the proverbial (one-up you) that we had Indian in our family— which explained the creamy light skin and long semi-straight hair of our elders. I always wandered exactly where my family came from. What was our "roots" story—minus all the plagiarism of Alex Haley's production?

Google Alex Haley's African-American hit series Roots and the book <u>scandal</u> (such a shame)

As a result, around 5 years after the passing of my great-great grandmother, I started to really realize how lucky I was to even know her. All the questions I should have asked her became so relevant. All that time I spent picking greens with her and playing in her bone straight hair, I could have asked so many questions about our family, our history.

I started to hunt down traces of my maternal family line based on oral history. The root of my family was a farm (or plantation) owned in Blooming Grove, Texas (part of Navarro county). I ended up driving an hour to the Corsicana Library because it had the most extensive genealogy department in that county.

I brought small pieces of information I had gathered from the internet by searching free databases like www.findagrave.com, (a trial free subscription to) www.ancestry.com, and a host of free US Census search engines. Along with some oral history and some very detailed obituaries found online, the main genealogist was able to piece my maternal line back to Navarro County just a little after 1824.

We found records of residence and marriage up to that point; no other "official" records were found; especially for mulattos and blacks. I did find out that my great-great-great-great-great grandparents were both mulattos; one from Mississippi, and the other from Alabama. To further find their origins, I know I'll have to hunt down some slave records from those states in particular. (This will probably be my next big venture.)

Traveling to that small town proved very fruitful. Besides paper records, the local genealogist recognized a name of one of my distant cousins (1st, 2nd, 3rd, I don't know). He fell on the same side as my great-great grandmother; as his dad was her brother. The women in the library told me he was still alive, but had just been hit by a car (at 80+ years old) two weeks before I got to town. I actually setup a meeting with him and his wife that following week.

He told me stories about my great-great-great grandmother Ada Hicks; whose nickname he confirmed as being "Ary." This was very important to me because conflicting consensus reports to listed her under different names. More mind blowing than that confirmation was the story he remembered about her.

He could vividly recall the large farm in Blooming Grove. The entire family would visit and all the kids would run around in the fields while "Ary" would sit on the porch yelling at them. "You niggas stop running around here." At which my newly found cousin said he would respond, "Shut up you ole white woman."

This was absolutely what I needed to hear, because before I made my way to Corsicana, my aunt—my great grandmother's sister—told me that exact same story, so I knew the story that I had just heard was legit.

To further fill in some holes, I took a chance and paid for the African Ancestry DNA kit—can you say expensive. It was like $300 for two tests. I took the "What's your mix" and the maternal line test. The first test broke down a racial mix of white, African, and American Indian. I was itching to see if that "Indian in my family" story would hold up.

Well, it didn't: 0% American Indian, 28% white, and 72% Sub-Saharan African. (I was really looking forward to those American Indian benefits those white people paid $5 to get with their registration on the Dawes Rolls. [Please Google the meaning behind "$5 Indian."])

Anyway, for both my parents to be regular black people, I thought my white percentage was a little high. But from the pamphlet for African Ancestry, it said that on average, an African American has about 25% white in them. I'm assuming this is from white male slave masters raping black slave women. The African Ancestry pamphlet went on even further to explain that they find European ancestry for about 30% of the paternal lineages they trace, regardless of ethnicity or skin color.

My maternal linage test came back to Sierra Leon; meaning that there is a very strong chance genetically that my slave mother was a Mende woman who took that horrible boat ride over here from Sierra Leon. I found that the list of other African Americans that hail from that same line were Martin Luther King, Corretta S. King, Isaiah Washington, India Arie, Michael K. Williams, and Mya Angelo (whom I always felt reminded me of my great grandmother).

Further research into the slaving of the people of Sierra Leon lead me to the boat Amistad. It was these same people, slaves that were captured from Sierra Leon, that over took a slave ship and went to court for their freedom and actually returned back to Africa. (It made me want to watch the movie all over again with a different eye.)

I found more interesting facts about the Mende people through their art history. The Mende people migrated to the coast of Sierra Leon from the other side of Africa [Sudan area—

making me a true member of the Nigrito people] around 200-1500 AD. Through linguistic and cultural traits they are linked to the decedents of the 13th century Mali Empire.

I decided to also take a comparative test from Ancestry.com—which is cheaper and gives and more detailed breakdown of your mix of nationalities. Although it didn't include the maternal line information, indicating my slave-mother's location. Months later, I submitted and received my results from Ancestry DNA: 78% African (24% Ivory Coast/Ghana; 22% Nigeria; 15% Cameroon/Congo; 6% Senegal, 4% Bantu, 3% Benin/Togo, 2% Mali, 2% South-central Hunter-gatherer); 21% Europe (17% Ireland, 3% Great Britain, 1% Iberian Peninsula); 1% Central Asia [around Afghanistan]. Talk about eye opening. (With the 17% Ireland, I can see my great-great-great grandfather being a white man with a red mustache; as my mama and cousin had told me years ago.)

After finding all of this out, I felt this gaping hole of the full image of myself filling in with every bit of knowledge of my family and lineage. It also felt rewarding because it took me a long time to get this collective information pieced together. I seriously tried one other time to collect info on my family right before I entered college. Every time I tried, I got a few pieces together; but nothing like this last push.

I encourage you to do some digging into your own family history. Try to get in touch with older members of your family. Better yet, get their memories on video tape before it's too late. Learning more and more about yourself through your family can help you draw a better picture of your identity past and present.

YouTube "Black Slaves, Red Masters"

(Find out the truth behind the Indian in the black family line: most "civilized" Indians owned black slaves! How many high school and college history school books do you read that in?)

A REFLECTION OF I AM:

Physics defines a reflection as the change in direction of a wave front at an interface between two different media so that the wave front returns into the medium from which it originated.

I am the reflection of the creator; mother of all men: black, white, yellow, brown

& science has rendered concordance with this as fact.

I am as brown as the Earth; yielding life, joy, and spiritual enlightenment.

My love is strong, is pure, is giving, is receiving, is patient, is willing, but forgive me dear Lord when I say:

I am so sick of this skinny ass white woman herald as the standard of beauty, & here lately her booty has been protruding,

Oh so now she big booty Judy, but 400 years ago mine was made a spectacle–shout-out to Sara Bartan, you the original mama.

& here lately her lips have been ballooning—Kylie Jenner syndrome I suppose.

& here lately her skin has been marooning—Snookie

& her Joes looking more and more like my bros, and her hairstyles a lil more urban—she must be taking notes from Rachel Dolezal.

& here lately her slang has gotten a lil loose—Iggy Azela with that fake black accent.

I hear them tell of this divine story of how God made man. This Adam and Eve couple portrayed in the media are a trip; shaped from clay but pale and opaque. All the while, my skin bares the real truth; holding all the colors of the world in one flesh and she (white eve) can bare nothing, yet one story spread wide and the other shunned.

White People and Why You think They tha Shit: Misconceptions Debunked

---

YouTube "Karma performed by Dominque Christina"

Welfare baby! Food stamp Queen! Derogatory right? Do you automatically think about a black single-baby mama? Well, let me tell you about the lie my mama let me in on. Since I was little, while we collected our WIC and food stamps, she let me know that this system wasn't created for us. She let me know that there were more white people using these programs than blacks. Who did you think is the majority on assistance? Clue: it ain't black people or brown people for that matter; but white people. But, you probably thought otherwise.

YouTube "Shahrazad Ali Speaks P.2 of 2" (pay attention @ 6 minute mark) **also watch the film *Claudine*** (to further understand what Ali is taking about)

I have visited high school classrooms where black kids have this skewed idea that all white people are well-off; and that they don't struggle financially, academically, or in any kind of the same ways that black people do. It's crazy how well the system has painted this fraud of a portrait.

Black kids have this *Leave it to Beaver* depiction of even average white people in America. The danger in this idea of the "perfect white situation" lies in the comparison of your own actual situation and that of some false white society. White people are not perfect—they have problems, average everyday problems like you and I (except the fear of getting shot in the street by the police or Gorge Zimmerman number two hunting them down in their own neighborhood); just like we have black folk problems and somewhat truthful stereotypes, so do they. Y'all know what I'm talking about. When you hear those type of stories in the news and you know it's a white person crime— shooter killed a family member and put them in the freezer, armed shooter kills multiple civilians before cops calmly detain him (because if he was black he would've been shot down for waving a sandwich in the air).

The problem with black kids thinking that white people are perfect is the same problem with white kids thinking that black people are all generally criminals, poor, uneducated, etc. Everyone sees a false sense of superiority in being white. As a black kid, you may begin to think that you're less than the next white person. Vice versa, a white person who believes all the stereotypes of black people assumes that a black person's worth is beneath them or that whites have a higher innate moral/ethical standard. Both positions are bullshit. Any person's worth should be evaluated on a case by case basis and solely grounded on their character and actions.

To all my #YBAs, know that the majority of white people are struggling at the same degree that we are, in most aspects. The Huffington Post reported in an article titled "80 Percent of U.S. Adults Face Near-Poverty" (updated 9/27/2013) that more than 19 million white people fall below the poverty line for a family of four, double the number of blacks. One of the most eye opening statistics of the article is that for the first time since 1975, poverty-stricken white single mother homes equaled in numbers of black homes due to jobless and a higher rate of out of wed-lock births among whites.

Despite what is thought, the welfare system largely excluded black people in its beginnings. In 1931, only 3% of welfare recipients were black. Dorothy Roberts cites in her excerpt of "Welfare and the Problem of Black Citizenship" that through the National Welfare Rights Organization movement, the welfare caseload moved from being 86% white recipients to having 46% non-white recipients by 1967.

Today we still find that the white population is the largest recipients of food stamps—although this has been mislabeled as a black thing. 2013 polls show that 40.2% of that that receive this aid are white, 25.7% are black, and 10.3% are Hispanic. You hear blacks and Hispanics used in a slur form when politicians talk about these types of programs when we aren't the majority consumers.

Now, what hasn't been a big part of the conversation has been the large organized white crime robbing this very system. On February 15, 2015, thirty white men and women were arrested in Brushton, NY. A white store owner allowed the criminals to use their food stamps to traffic a street exchange rate. He was also arrested; as it was the store owners second time getting arrested for such behavior. All other defendants were charged with second degree criminal use of a public card and petty larceny; and we all know had they been black, they would've been serving federal time somewhere for 10 plus years.

White people are just as criminally inclined as any other race. Again to my #YBAs, know that they don't have anything on you **unless** you fall for the banana in the tailpipe. I can't lie, I fell for it in high school. By the time I got to college, and had no choice but to surround myself with a large amount of "privileged" white kids, I found out just how average/dumb a lot of them were (and it was no coincidence that the dumb ones were the ones that seemed to be so cocky).

I mean, I was blown away. I thought I was going to be so freaking far behind in all my college classes. But when group-work projects came, I found out how much these kids didn't know and how lazy they were. Not only that, but a lot of them were from bottom-level middle class homes—they were just talking/walking the walk; but were struggling financially and academically, as well. Those with trust-funds needed them because they had no common sense to fall back on.

We have this perception that white people are just brilliant and have it all figured out. Well, the truth is, we're not too far behind them, number wise. The mainstream media likes to promulgate that there are more black men in prison than college; well, that's a lie. Reports from 2002 by the Department of Education reported that more black men were enrolled in postsecondary education than were in prison or jail. But come to find out, this reality was probably a long standing truth many years before. Ivory Toldson—an associate Professor at Howard—found that a number of colleges weren't reporting their black male enrollment to the Justice Policy Institute. Specifically, by leaving HBCUs out of the survey, the resulting report was centered on limited data.

By 2009, after more colleges were included in the survey numbers, there was an estimated 600,000 more black male postsecondary presence than black males in prison and jail. (See the games they play when they control and manipulate the information?) Continuing on the topic of blacks in education versus that of whites, we find that black women enroll in college more than any race and gender in the US as of 2011. [Please YouTube "Black women are ranked the most educated group" (length 2:32 min).]

The skewed media projection in America points a consistent finger at black and brown youth alike in association with criminal activity while sweeping the white-deranged criminal under the rug. In 2015, the white male was deemed the #1 terrorist in America based on mass shootings, hostage situations, and the like. Bump ISIS, I'm more afraid of a crazy white man shooting up my local church, movie theatre, or park.

Peter Gelling in his article "White Americans are the biggest terror threat in the United States" writes that more people have died at the hands of right-wing groups than by Muslim extremists. You got white extremists like the Bundy family taking over government buildings with guns, you got random public shooting at movie theatres and schools, you got rich white kids with "affluenza" committing multiple vehicular homicides; and you got white boys shooting up churches full of black people after bible study. I mean, the list goes on and nobody seems to think there's a problem here.

I mean really, what's the root cause? In general terms, minorities usually commit crimes of circumstance and survival. "I ain't got no $, go rob somebody with some $." But what in the hell is going on in the white community?

Your thoughts:

_____

_____

_____

_____

_____

_____

_____

_____

The Apparent Double Standard

YouTube "Amandla Stenberg: Don't Cash Crop on my Cornrows"

In a time of Kylie Jenners, Riff-Raffs, Iggys, and Justin Timberlakes, where in the world am I supposed to be black? If I do me and engage in all the habits and culturalisms of my people, I'm viewed as ghetto or ratchet. White people even get a little scared. But, when Becky and Tom mimic me, they're freaking trendsetters and can open several businesses or gain endorsements and get paid to "act black."

In 2016, this is where we are. Black culture is the shit! It's marketable; and, it's universal. It just isn't benefiting our #YBAs any. White people are turning black right in front of our very eyes! Mainstream society acts like it's not an artificial movement (via surgery) occurring; and, we as black people aren't getting any credit for the style these culture vultures are jacking.

Soundtrack "White Privilege" (1 & 2) by Macklemore and Ryan Lewis

---

White people are tanning themselves to a golden brown (sometimes orange), they are buying thick lips, buying black girl booties; and some of the younger white kids think that they can greet you with a "my nigga." They have assumed our culture, prepackaged it, and think that they have a stake in it. I can't help but wonder if this is a fad; and if they will move on to the next cultured people and commercialize their ethnic identifiers. Or, have they just leached on to us and won't quit until all of our swag, speech, and very essence is sucked dry? I mean, these days blackness even comes in a bottle [Google the drug Melanotan 2].

I'm convinced that the world just prefers the watered down version of us because they can't handle us in our Divine fullness. I mean as black people, we are the only race that has to apologize for being "who" and "what" we are. White people seem to only be able to take us in doses. [When you're too real: YouTube "Africans the only pure human beings."]

Kylie Jenner and Justine Beiber sport some ratty looking dreadlocks and are coined "trendy;" but, Zendaya adorns a head of perfect faux locks and is deemed a pothead. Beyonce performs at the Super Bowl dressed in Black Panther regalia commemorating their 50th anniversary; and it's a controversy. Kendrick Lamar pretty much makes everybody piss their pants during his 2016 Grammy performance because of his straight forward lyrics and visuals. Meanwhile, the 2016 Oscars committee found it irrelevant to nominate not one actor of color.

In the sports arena, our black athleticism continues to be deride with an undertone of jealousy and spiteful admiration. Richard Sherman—a 4.0 Ivy League graduate (with no criminal record)—is heralded a "thug" because he boasts about his undisputed records on the football field; while white hockey players wait for the start of their game; only to push the puck aside and have an all-out brawl. Serena Williams is constantly being bullied over her "bulky" and "muscular" body image by white commentators (only mad because she continues to BODY the frail young white girls she plays). [Google Serena's New York Magazine Fashion issue. See that split; that's a bad chick.] And LeBron James unknowingly allows Vogue Magazine (cover issue April 2008) to compare him to an ape. [There's a deep connection to this cover and the original movie poster for King Kong; which is a derogatory film based on the black boxer Jack Johnson. Please Google.] When we make something look good and we do it with ease, we get criticized and ridiculed for it. But once a white person comes along and does the same thing, it's the coolest thing since sliced bread (and they're really oh so lame).

We take the ordinary and make it extraordinary in everything we do. The game of basketball use to be a simple dribble, pass, and shoot technique. That is until we started flying (dunking). Because majority of the other players couldn't match this level of athleticism, a ban on dunking was proposed at the NBA level and was executed on the NCAA level. Likewise, in football, the ability to literally hurdle over your opponent was frown upon. In the ice skating arena, a black woman by the name of Surya Bonaly continuously dealt with gender and race discrimination while kicking ass on the rink [YouTube "How back flipping black figure skater Surya Bonaly changed sports forever].

Outside of sports, just recently, Malia Obama announced her acceptance into Harvard; and that she would take one year off before entering school. The internet went crazy with accusations that she only got in because of her family's influence; combined with affirmative action. Nobody said two shits about the drunken Bush twins and their apparent white privilege, but I digress.

We live by a double edged sword; and if we don't boldly reclaim our greatness, our #YBAs won't know who they are and what our people have cultivated for them. Case in point, rapper Lil Kim is now a white girl, SMH! She has turned herself into an imitation of a Kardashian, which in turn, is an imitation of a black girl. So now, Lil Kim is like 2X removed from her original blackness. [Google picture of before and after of Lil Kim.] Lord help us!

Chapter Notes:

_____

_____

_____

_____

_____

_____

_____

_____

_____

_____

_____

_____

_____

_____

_____

_____

_____

The Next Chapter is Yours to Write:

"The absence of evidence is not the evidence of absence."

-Dr. Carl Sagan

In general, the most important lesson I've learned is to learn from others. If I had to give a sound-bite of advice it would be: don't make the same mistakes that others close to you have; learning from a mistake that you don't have to live through is the cheapest lesson. Secondly, don't rush to grow up so quickly; be a kid for as long as possible.

The true worries of adulthood **suck**, especially when you are ill prepared for them or you make huge mistakes that set you back in achieving your ultimate goals. Once you have set yourself back, it becomes even harder to deal with the new worries and challenges because you have further complicated them with old baggage.

Now when I say stay a kid, I don't mean do foolish things, or maintain a childish attitude. Be responsible. Research and make informed decisions, but don't put yourself in positions where you HAVE to deal with adult situations as a teenager (typical examples: running away/moving out of a stable home because "you wanna be grown," getting pregnant early, starting substance abuse because of peer pressure) Doing unnecessary things create unnecessary bills and can further ruin your chances of living out your potential.

Through all the propaganda and bullshit, the truth is, we are in a new age of slavery. As a #YBA of this generation, you have a revolutionary fight ahead of you. The dynamic of the game has changed. It's not just black and white any more. You see, "the system" is playing everybody: the white people at your job telling you what to do aren't necessarily the "overseers"; just the new age house-niggers. As much power as you think they have, they don't really have. Black people (all of us) still play the role of "field niggas" (along with other minority groups) until

197

we—through your generation—gain a little purpose and start a little rebellion (led by free thinking). It's time to wake up!

The system only has two plans for #YBAs: 1) either it educates you just enough for prison; or, 2) it provides you with quasi-education suitable for college. With either option, you service their purpose: 1) you end up in a prison providing goods for corporations under free slave-labor, which they sell for profit or 2) you end up graduating from college with debt and look to get employed for mediocre pay using your intellect to further their corporate revenue. BUT, once this generation of #YBAs learn to operate on their own dreams, these old options die.

I feel indebted to all #YBAs. During my last year in high school, throughout college and grad school, I neglected my two younger brothers to a certain degree because I was really trying to figure stuff out (like getting into and finishing college, getting a real job, learning how to use $ effectively, etc.). As a result, my brothers kind of got caught up and I left them in the wind without that big sister eye watching over them. But, for my nieces and nephew and mentee #YBAs, I promise to be an agent of change for the betterment of our black youth. I also challenge others to do the same, especially those in the 25-35 age range. It's a trickle-down effect. Our entire community has a responsibility to aid our little brothers and sisters, but ultimately it's up to each #YBA.

To start **your** journey, you must first, forgive yourself and your family members, be bold in trying to better yourself through positive changes, celebrate your failures as a lesson learned, strive to better yourself by any means necessary, and GO AFTER WHAT YOU WANT! Dream bigger than your beginning. This book in no way is all-inclusive of the tasks and the possibilities you will have to assess to reach your goals in life. There are several holes in the information that I have presented; you have to go through life and arm yourself through self-knowledge (based on true history) and investigation in order to fill those holes. I am far from an expert in most of the ideals I have discussed, but they are things that I wish someone would have pointed out to me earlier on in my development. I hope that this information at least sparks several fires and plants multiple seeds for you in your journey of redefining what it means to be Young, Black, and American.

Back in the Gap

These are classics that set records for blacks and have become a form of reference

Influential and Pivotal Movies in Black America

The Color Purple

Hollywood Shuffle

Fresh

South Central

Malcolm X

Selma

Roots

The Book of Negros (DVD set also a book)

Brewster's Place

Boys in the Hood

Claudine

School Daze

Friday

Coming to America

Their Eyes Were Watching God

American Gangster

Do the Right Thing

Shaft

Mississippi Burning

Menace to Society

Cleopatra

New Jack City

Eve's Bayou

Cooley High

Krush Groove

Lean On Me

Stormy Weather

The Dorothy Dandridge Story

The Sally Hemmings Story

Carmen Jones

A Raisin in the Sun

Blacula	Straight Outta Compton
Amistad	Baby Boy
Crooklyn	Lady Sings the Blues
Super Fly	The Book of Negros
Coffy	Ali
Foxy Brown	Imitation of Life
Cleopatra Jones	Vampire in Brooklyn
Friday	

Must See Documentaries

Hidden Colors (1, 2, 3, & 4)

Out of Darkness

Bleaching Black Culture

Black Panthers: The Vanguard

Secrets of the Pyramids

YouTube "Dr. Ivan Sertima The Ancient High Science—The Golden Age of the Moor

"Africans in Early Europe—Dr. Ivan Van Sertima"

Broader Span of Music/Poetry

It is imperative that you listen to more than what is "allowed" on the radio these days. Your mind needs constant stimulation and thought provoking ideas; other than sex, drugs, and thug mentality. Again, I'm not claiming to not like the commercial hip hop and R&B on the radio; but I can't deal with listening to it ALL THE TIME. Here's a little relief from the daily program (google and YouTube these artists):

Sunni Patterson

LaCrae

Sa-Roc

Jacki Hill Perry

Gemstone

Brook Yung

Bishop Nurhu

Oddisee

Los King

Mick Jenkins

Leon Brigdes

Logic

Audra Day

Appendix A

The Proliferation of For-Profit Prisons: The Modern Day Slave Trade

Porscha Kelley

Circa 2010

Introduction

Buy... sell... redistribute... and exclude. The never-ending cycle of capitalism in the U.S. free-market economy treats every discernible tangible and intangible object as a commodity, including freedom. The government has proved to be the most efficient and effective agent in manufacturing, restricting, and selling freedom. With the claims of promoting life, liberty, and the pursuit of happiness, the government utilizes punishment and the open market to promote the interests of the privileged and swell the pockets of the influential. From the time the first indentured servant reached the shores of the New World, the tangible product derived from the construction of punishment—free labor—has driven our economy at the lowest possible cost. Those fortunate enough to gain profit from this free labor further enlarged their piece of the economic pie once the system of American slavery began to overshadow the indentured servant model.

Slavery was reflected in the letter of the law and became the economic buoy of the South. After its abolishment, the U.S. criminal justice system was further compromised and manipulated in order to supply the south with no-wage labor. The enforcement of Black Codes became a 'justified' institution of slavery through the use of the penal system. As a byproduct, the state government and private business owners were again able to capitalize upon involuntary black labor. Even as outwardly racist laws were pushed out of practice, the criminalization of actions tied to civil upheaval and the ever-evolving war on drugs (with its main target being disenfranchised minorities) sparked a new era of the black slave trade. The primary construction and operation of this transition existed through the prison system. The young black prisoner emerged as the ultimate commodity; bought and sold by the bed, per day.

While appealing to public fear of crime, politicians and businessmen, alike, garner huge benefits and profits from the construction, finance, and services provided to the prison system (Christie 2000). The contracts acquired in prison construction alone constitute a $4-6 billon a year business. Furthermore, the privation of the prison business has distinctly emphasized the continued exploitation of economically and politically deficient members of society in order to promote financial gain; as slavery is still alive and well in America, deeply entrenched in business and government. The black body and the sale of available space are the products bought, sold, and redistributed in the private prison market.

Early Forms of Punishment and Profit

The private prison market was developed in the mid-1980s, approximately around 1984—a time when public sector prisons started to see exponential growth in its non-violent offender population. Political figureheads sought a quick and relatively solvent alternative; correctional departments at the local, state, and federal level utilized the option of contracting private sector facilities to house the surplus of prisoners. An impressive number of private facilities opened during the 1990s with a total of 158 facilities operating in 30 states, the District of Columbia, and Puerto Rico, but this system could not exist without the forerunners of for-profit imprisonment.

As early as the idea of private custody became a good to be sold, the infant model of the private contractor existed. Jeremy Bentham—an advocate of utilitarianism—thought of himself as a private prison contractor; his inception of the 'Panoptican' was pitched as a contract proposal for hire to construct, administer, and manage prisons. His circular model was offered as a "cost-efficient means of mitigating risk by enabling a small number of guards to supervise a large number of convicts via its novel design" (Hallett 2009, p 116). Venture capitalists have since engaged in the market of prisoner management.

The English system of transportation, created by private merchant shippers of the 17th century, involved the exporting of convicted criminals to North American and Australian plantations for indentured labor. These merchants made profit from the selling of convict labor to the colonies; here, "racialized caste systems imposed varying degrees of servitude" among those subjected to labor (i.e. the "Christian [white] servant" and the Negro). This historical characteristic of distinction between the two laborers illustrates "how race, punishment, and profit have long been bound together in widely constructed, multi-national capitalistic schemes" (Hallett 2009, p 116). Later, slavery and the crime statutes of the U.S. began to overtly reflect this racial theme.

The primitive concept of privatized prison institutions was constructed around European workhouse models where private contractors reimbursed the state for use of its inmates to manufacture products to be sold on the open market. An early form of convict leasing agreements was established between the state and private entrepreneurs. In the 19th century, prisons were operating in the black, profiting from free labor; however, this free labor market was "rife with abusive, exploitive treatment of inmates and sweetheart contracting arrangements" (Culp 2005, p 421). In the 20th century, Progressive Era reforms abolished the use of contracted labor from prisons in most states; by the 1920s and 1930s many groups from the business community and organized labor unions argued that state-owned prisons "constituted unfair competition" and that "cheap convict labor depressed the wages of free workers" (Culp 2005, p 421). Consequently, by 1940, almost every state banned the importation of prison-made goods, eroding the "old privatization era" (Culp 2005, p 421). However, the use of cheap labor still persisted and the government did its part in assuring an abundant supply of prison laborers.

The Convict Leasing System

The mass imprisonment of black males, subject to the post-bellum southern penal system, was due to the Black Codes of the South, which mirrored slave codes. Arrests made under these terms resulted in drones of black men inducted into chain gangs or sold into private custody via the convict leasing system. Records of working conditions and treatment suffered imply that a black man, especial one from the South, faired a better involuntary working life under the system of slavery than under the convict leasing system (Davis 2000).

One of the secondary forms of privatized supervision was born out of the legislation which abolished slavery and enabled the convict leasing system to persist. The post-bellum labor shortage in the South, whose economic life thrived on intensive agricultural labor, facilitated white supremacy ideology and the continuation of racialized forced labor. This labor shortage was engendered by three distinct occurrences: 1) the abolition of slavery, 2) the dissipated system of indentured servitude, and 3) the depleted supply of able-bodied worker as a result of the Civil War, leaving many men killed or maimed (Hallett 2009).

Operators of the American system of slavery benefited, unequivocally, from the involuntary service of Africans and African Americans, whose labor greatly surpassed that of the white indentured servant. The slavery system was so lucrative that the states would not and could not completely let it die. In fact, "the very instrument of slavery's abolition in the United States, the 13th Amendment to the U.S. Constitution, also authorized the 'involuntary servitude' of prisoners as a punishment for crime" (Hallett 2009, p 117). The convict leasing system and the latter privatized prison labor market was enabled through a loophole in the 13th Amendment, which states:

> Neither slavery nor involuntary servitude, except as a punishment for crime whereof the party shall have been duly convicted, shall exist within the United States, or any place subject to their jurisdiction. Congress shall have power to enforce this article by appropriate legislation (U.S. Constitution, 13th Amendment).

It is less than coincidental that the majority of those who find themselves convicted under our justice system and subject to involuntary servitude are ancestral decedents of those who were reluctantly freed from the institution of slavery. Black males are incarcerated at a rate eight times higher than white males in the U.S., largely characterized by the "imprisonment of minority males in the prime of their lives," during the most optional time of productivity, for non-violent drug crime (Hallett 2009, p 118). In the United States "dispossession affects people of color and 'aliens' in far greater proportion than whites" (Hallett 2009, p 121); the correlation between the war on drugs and the proliferation of private prisons "cannot be understood outside of the context of race" (Hallett 2009, p 123). Historically the racial criterion of dispossession has been the "source of exploitative profits in the past" (Hallett 2009, p 123).

Not only have slave-like conditions been allowed through the 13th Amendment, but judgment from the highest court in the land has constituted the reduction of "constitutional associational rights" of prisoners (Jones v. North Carolina). This stance is 'justified' by the theoretical deduction that "after receiving a fair trial and sentence, [prisoners] have forfeited fundamental rights and freedoms because of the crimes they committed" (Kang 2009, p146). This finding terminates a prisoner's claim to basic protections of the law, including the freedom of association and the right to organize (especially with the intent to strike); such an existence characterizes the livelihood of a new age slave of the state (Ruffin v. Common Wealth).

This secondary form of 'justified' slavery—taking the form of punishment for criminal mischief—had no obligation to maintain the worker/prisoner because the system reflected no form of ownership by those leasing convict labor nor did the system appreciate the individual skill capacity of each prisoner. Since those companies and individuals leasing out the labor of convicts had no other loyalties to the prisoners, working conditions were extremely brutal, including the receipt of vicious punishment for slow work (lashing with whips), constant disparagement (being called Nigger, Boy, Coon, etc.), and exposure to severe elements (prisoners consistently died from sunstroke, pneumonia, and/or frostbite). The life span for a prisoner under the convict leasing system was significantly shorter than that of a southern slave (Trulson & Marquart 2009).

The Proliferation of Private Prisons

The birth of the custody privatization arose by the start of the 1970s with the system looking a bit differently. Instead of the state leasing and receiving funds for the labor of prisoners, within the new system of prison privatization, "private entities would be paid by the state to keep prisoners in custody" (Culp 2005, p 422). Community Corrections Acts were adopted by 25 states which transferred resources from state departments of corrections to local authorities to facilitate community residential facilities to low-level offenders. Accordingly, many jurisdictions found it easier to delegate this task to private contractors who operated low-custody facilities. The hand of the free market was at work and business minded goals handcuffed government responsibilities at a pretty penny.

Three distinct streams created a framework, which converged and diverged, birthing the emergence and decline of private prisons on a national level; including the amount of problems experienced with public sector prisons, including policies and politics. The prison population began to grow, and then skyrocket by the mid-1970s placing a large strain on government and public resources, especially around the late 90s when the prison population ballooned to more than 1.3 million. As a late reaction to 'tough on crime' crusades and the growing non-violent offender pool quickly replicating, "many states tried to build their way out of the problem" (Culp 2005, p 419). From 1979-1995, about 256 state facilities were built. Consequently, spending on prisons grew from $5 billion to $40 billion between the late 1970s to the mid-1990s, averaging about $2 billion a year by the 1990s (Culp 2005). The states' development time for establishing new public prisons ranged from four to five years, partly due to the extensive process of gaining voter approval of construction bonds.

Specifically referring to the birth of the private prison industry, the war on drugs produced an abundant supply of prisoners. While politicians steadily pushed 'tough on crime' initiatives, non-violent offenders filtered into prison at an exponential rate; states could not provide an adequate amount of bed space in the public prison sector. Our public prison system beginning to burst at is seams as a result of the over criminalization of offenses that disproportionately profiled and sentenced minority males. Specifically referring to the 1980's war on drugs, black and Hispanic youth were overtly targeted on urban streets and taken into custody in very large groups (Hangartner, 1994).

The United States' addiction to imprisonment has made its mark; as the National Council on Crime and Delinquency (2006) found that the U.S. incarceration rate is four times the world average and that our crime rate does not accurately account for this incarceration rate. Minorities are aberrantly overrepresented in the prison population, especially considering their numeric make up of the U.S. general population. Efforts in facilitating the incarceration of such a large pool of offenders, without regard to a diminishing effect, resulted in the undesirable responsibility of housing this abundance of offenders. Consequently, state and federal budgets were not equipped to handle such an influx of prisoners. A 2007 report by Pew Charitable Trust estimated that over the following five years the U.S. may need over $27.5 billion surplus to accommodate prison expansion and operations. Consequently, a viable alternative was explored, in particular private prisons.

The Rise and Stall of Private Prisons

It is theorized that the inception of private prison facilities has been made possible through policy-making perspectives: policy windows, advocacy coalitions, sub-governments, and disjointed incrementalism among others. These aspects coalesced and formed a system of multiple streams allowing for the emergence of privatized custody arrangements (Kingdon 2003). By the late 1980s, a policy window had opened. Policy windows are available when the following occurs: a problem captures the attention of government officials; an alternative practice/policy is suggested and readily available; and political attitudes and administration ebb and flow along with public opinion (Kingdon 2003). Prison overcrowding and a litany of class action suits claiming unconstitutional treatment allowed for think tanks and political action that embraced the use of private custody contracting.

As the population in both federal and state facilities skyrocketed, public prisons found themselves operating profusely over capacity. By the latter end of 1989, the federal prison population had reached 190% of its capacity and 24 states were operating public prisons at 125-150% of their capacity (Culp 2005). By 1980, over two-thirds of the states were operating prisons under federal court orders and consent decrees; this number grew to 80% by 1992 (Culp 2005). The overcrowding and inhumane conditions of the U.S. prison system sparked public attention (via riots); inviting federal court intervention of day-to-day prison management affairs. This was a process made possible in light of the corruption, sandal, and overcrowded conditions like those presented in the 1982 case of Grubbs v. Bradley in Tennessee.

Regarding claims of inhumane conditions, the 1982 Ruiz v. Estelle decision incited mandated structural and operational changes in the Texas prison system, ballooning public prison operating costs tenfold between the years of 1980-1994. As a consequence, limitations were set on prison populations in a need to curtail the large capital expenditures of the big business of prison. This generated a great pressure to "locate funds for new facilities and to intensify the search for alternative forms of sentencing and custody" (Feeley & Rubin 1998, p 380). A policy window for prison privatization had materialized.

Complications created an environment conducive to change and allowed the operation of the first private prison in the country. In 1982, the Corrections Corporation of America (CCA) was formed by Thomas Beasley (political figurehead), Doctor Crants (reality developer), Jack Massey (the founder of American Hospital Supply of America), and Lucius Burch (a venture capitalist). In 1988, CCA moved on the opportunity to supply custody services to a government entity, the Immigration and Naturalization Service (INS). The CCA's bid to supply a 350-bed detention facility for the bounty of illegal aliens in Houston, Texas was accepted by the INS. CCA had the facility ready by April 1984 of the following year. That same year, CCA secured a state contract in Tennessee, near Chattanooga, to operate a county-run prison, becoming the first private prison operator in the U.S.

Political Coalition

Sub-government and advocacy coalitions worked hand-in-hand to cement grassroots efforts of constructing a private prison market; a political shift most advanced these interests. A political ideology change emerged with the election and actions of Ronald Reagan in 1980, with legislative action in issuing Reform 88, constructing the Grace Commission panel, and redrafting the Office of Management and Budget Circular A 76, regarding the performance of commercial activities (Culp 2005). Reagan essentially set forth a path concentrated on improving government performance and efficiency through the use of the private sector, contracted services. Advocacy coalitions help promote policy changes during policy windows. This group of actors, usually comprised from a variety of government and private organizations, operate under core beliefs—the "lowest common denominator" of shared interests—and unites "disparate organizations and individuals from multiple jurisdictions to advance (or suppress) public policy" (Culp 2005, p 415).

The Reagan Era revived the "Americanization of Dixie" where the continual use of Nixon's "Southern strategy" to demobilize a minority electoral base and limit American democracy (Wood 2007, p 228). The imprisonment of black people for political and economic purposes was accomplished by "[criminalizing] where possible" and "[demonizing] where not" (Wood 2007, p

213

229). The criminal justice system was used to reinforce social order transcendent from slavery, convict leasing, chain gangs, to the buying and selling of private custody for prisoners. This argument is well illustrated during America's most explosive "correctional expansion"; which coincidentally occurred during periods of racial and civil unrest—directly following the abolishment of slavery, civil rights act, and the war on drugs (Wood 2007, p 229). Politicians openly championed campaigns against 'dangerous classes' coupling race and crime, making them synonymous.

The South has maintained fertile ground for racialized prison systems to exist where prisoners are subject to the market as a commodity and continue to be exploited for profit (Wood 2007). Even when the push for privatization began to stall, trailblazing states like Texas, Tennessee, and Oklahoma had several private facilities operating within their state lines. Soon Mississippi, Georgia, and Virginia followed suit, accounting for a large majority of the privative adult prisons.

As prison overcrowding became the causation of a public financing dilemma, coalitions in favor of prison privatization began to push the idea that the "[government's] monopoly of services had the net effect of lower quality and higher costs" (Culp 2005, p 424). Public managers were advocated to include private entities in service delivery to increase efficiency and innovation. Even though several bodies of research, including a U.S. General Accounting Office meta-analysis (1996), have not been able to definitively show that either prison system, public or private, is able to provide superior costs or better conditions of confinement, state and local officials were regularly entertaining the expansion of prison privatization at professional conferences around the country.

By 1996, Democratic, Republican, and Libertarian parties were all endorsing the idea of contracting with the private sector. The number of bed spaces under contract steadily increased from 1990-1999, growing from 15,300 beds to 145,160 beds (Culp 2005).But as the millennium approached, the growth rate of the private prison market began to decline and level off. At this time, "the private prison industry had captured only a 5% market share of total U.S. prison bed space" (Culp 2005, p 413).

The sub-government aspect of Kingdon's (2003) multiple stream theory highlights the influence of "individuals and small groups at the jurisdictional level" (Culp 2005, p 415), those in an elite circle of government bureaucracies and agencies (like bureau chiefs, administrators, private contractors, and state/local government officials) gain from the allocation of public resources. Within this closed circle, new ideas are initiated and able to garner "the necessary political support to get their ideas enacted into law by state legislatures" (Culp 2005, p 415). Taxpayer money is recklessly poured into these ill-developed ventures—public and private—at the expense of the public, but usually to the benefit of those policy-makers within those closed circles (Hallett 2009). The two leading private entities whom specialize in private custody (CCA and Wackenhut) had founders, directors, and board members with intimate ties to the Secret Service, FBI, CIA, and several other high profile agencies, not to mention many influential political figureheads at the state and federal level (Wood 2007). This enabled both companies to not only flex their "wield political influence," but to "insert themselves directly or indirectly into the corrections policy-making process" (Wood 2007, p 232).

The Business of Private Prisons

As prisoners became a commodity, companies supplying private custody, like CCA and Wackenhut, became "promising investment-objects" on the stock market (Christie 2000, p 118). Companies providing private custody like CCA and Wackenhut (also known as Geo Group) together control approximately 75% of the private prison market (Pelaez 2008). With estimates that Wackenhut could cut about 15% from every $50 that the government used to feed, clothe, and guard an inmate, we see that room for profit trumps quality and assurance of confinement. This mentality all too clearly mirrors that of the southern slave plantation where the very minimum amount of car to sustain life of said slave became the adequate investment in assurance of profit.

The business side of prison, the privatized market in particular, views and utilizes the black male body as a dispensable commodity—an items to be bartered for as a means to an end, financial gain. Black men and a number of poor minorities are the target of modern enslavement by way of penal infractions and long stints of prison. Texas' Private facilities, for example, generate about $80 million annually (Pelaez 2008).

Private companies have an economic interest in holding custody of inmates as long as possible (Davis 2005). Although good behavior can be accumulated in CCA facilities (accounting for a reduced sentence), but in efforts to keep profits high, inmates at these facilities can get 30 days added to their sentence for any infraction; not surprisingly, CCA inmates have been known to loss "good behavior time" at a rate eight times higher than inmates of a state prison (Pelaez 2008).

The "prison industry complex" condones a legal market for slave labor to persist in our current open market—prison work operates as a secondary good resulting from the buying and selling of bed space. By 2008, thirty-seven states legalized the ability for privately held companies to contract prison labor; the list of subscriber includes large market shareholders of their specialty like Microsoft, Hewlett-Packard, Revlon, Texas Instrument, and Macy's (Pelaez 2008). In state facilities, inmates may receive as little as 17 cents per hour for their efforts, totaling about $20 per week. CCA holds the title for the highest paying private corporation paying out a generous 50 cents per hour for what is considered "highly skilled positions" (Pelaez 2008). Privatized prisons are profitable for all involved except the prisoner; in particular, Texas CCA operated private prisons have been known to offer "rent-a-cell" services where salesmen can receive anywhere from $2.50-5.50 per day per bed in which they can contract overcrowded out-of-state prisons.

Prison labor has also been lobbied for on the economic grounds of promoting prosperity for the greater economic growth of the U.S. It has been argued that with full participation of the prison population, the total productivity of the U.S. could increase by $20 billion a year (Kang 2009). The question is, to whose benefit, the public or those of the exclusive closed circles who influence such policy? In spite of ultimate kickbacks benefiting those most influential in creating and advocating such policy, this fiscal gain is argued to help subsidize the high operation costs of prison as they reach capacity and function on insufficient funds (Kang 2009).

The Stall and Campaign for Resurgence

The incrementalist perspective, in regards to policy-making, begins as more of a tactical process where corrections to past mistakes are made, unanticipated problems are circumvented, or clarifications are addressed to resolve pressing emergencies. This disjointed incrementalism was found to contribute too much of the state legislation passed in the late 1990s; placing the limitations on prison privation that may have led to its stall (based on reactions to day-to-day problems of private prison operations). Two particular characteristics of disjointed incrementalism which influenced policy change, one, a "limitation of analysis to few somewhat familiar policy alternatives" and, two, a "greater analytical preoccupation with ills to be remedied than positive goals to be sought" (Culp 2005, p 417).

With its expansion, private prisons begin to mirror that of public prisons; decreasing the incentives and initial reasoning behind privatization in the first place. Private prisons began to reflect the same management issues as it public counter-part including cases of escapees, lawsuits, corruption (involving conflicts of interests), and civil unrest amongst inmates. During the years of 1997-1999, the private prison system experienced several episodes of disarray leading to regulatory policies which essentially disintegrated its proposed advantage over the public corrections sector.

In 1997, a privately run prison detainee in Houston escaped; this episode was again repeated more than eight times in other areas of the country. Later on that year, inmates from a private prison in Ohio filed a class action suit against the CCA claiming that their civil rights were violated. Concurrently, a number of assaults on inmates and the Northeast Ohio Correctional Center (NEOCC) staff made news. Compounding the complications experienced by private prisons, mounting corruption amongst privatization board members and founders began to further taint private prisons' image including the investigation of

Dr. Charles Thomas. Thomas was investigated on the grounds that his service as the director of the CCA's real estate investment trust directly conflicted with his interests in serving on the Florida Correctional Privatization Commission and his influence in leading privatization research.

Legislative action soon followed. Because private prison custody personnel had no formal authority regarding runaways, "many states had to broaden legal definitions to include private prisons" in order to substantiate private prison agencies (Culp 2005, p 428). In addition, as a reaction to the number of escapees during the interstate transfer of inmates, private prisons were restricted—signaling a "preference for private prisons to operate solely as adjuncts to state prisons" (Culp 2005, p 430). Concerns of an over reliance on the private sector began to surface which led to legislation that placed caps on the use of privatized facilities (lower-security private prisons could not house more than 30% of total bed spaces state-wide) (Culp 2005). Private companies offering custody have an incentive to cut corners that may prohibit the proper performance of duties (Austin & Irwin 2001).

There exists a certain responsibility of the government to administer and oversee incarceration and ensure the upholding of the constitutional rights of inmates—a responsibility that questionably should not be delegated. Even though the private sector has experienced criticism regarding such shortcomings, a continual use of private facilities exists. In addition to the heavy reliance upon private prisons by the state, the federal government is undergoing expansion from which private prisons will be the primary beneficiaries.

The current direction of prison privatization is moving on to a global stage where the argument for the democratic 'common good' rests on a "condition of fiscal capacity, not social aspiration" (Hallett 2009, p 120). (The same argument essentially used to justify slavery in the South as a buoy of the economy and the livelihood of the country as a whole.) American corrections and security firms are actively biding for contracts in South Africa, Iraq, Israel, and Ireland.

After the events of September 11th and the war in Iraq, the federal government has integrated and reorganized the Immigration and Naturalization Service under the guise of the Bureau of Immigration and Customs Enforcement (ICE). This operation falls under the Department of Homeland Security—securing direct ties between incarceration and immigration. As the federal government further cracks down on criminal aliens, the fastest growing portion of the federal prison population, more low-security prisons will be needed. This will facilitate an expansion of the national prison system, specifically that which detains immigrants facing deportation.

Conclusion

For a substantial amount of time, the government has participated in; or acted as, a middleman during the bartering and/or selling of the human commodity, involuntary servitude. The African slave, the second class African American citizen, and the disenfranchised minority youth have all had their turn as the objects of exploitation on the black market of labor, copiloted by the government at every capacity. African slaves dominated the involuntary workforce until the forced end of slavery. The 'criminal' African American male soon substituted this population. In fact, by 2004, about 41% of the state and federal inmates in the country were black—an astonishing number considering that at that time African Americans made up about 12% of the U.S. general population (Harrison &

Beck 2005). At this current time of political warfare, the marginalized immigrant has been targeted and set to take the stage as the next hot commodity in the big business of privatized prison.

The cycle of buying, selling, redistributing, and excluding certain racial groups will never cease, especially when a willing and profitable market for their exploitation exists. The fact that the government is willing to play such an obvious role in such an unjust cycle is more than a little disturbing. The compromise of government responsibilities and the criminal justice system as a whole result in social and equitable disarray for our society in general. Our prison system, both public and private, has provided the perfect example of such a phenomena.

Reference

Austin, J., & Irwin, J. (2001). *It's about time: America's imprisonment binge*. Australia: Wadsworth.

Christie, N. (2000). *Crime control as industry: Towards gulags, Western style*. London: Routledge.

Culp, R. (2005). The Rise and Stall of Prison Privatization: An Integration of Policy Analysis Perspectives. *Criminal Justice Policy Review, 16,* 4, 412-442.

Davis, A.Y. (2000). *From the Convict Lease System to the Super-Max Prison*. States of Confinement: Policing, Detention, and Prison. New York: St. Martin's Press.

Feeley, M. M., & Rubin, E. L. (1998). *Judicial policy making and the modern state: How the courts reformed America's prisons*. New York: Cambridge University Press.

Hallett, M. (2009). Imagining the global corporate gulag: lessons from history and criminological theory. *Contemporary Justice Review, 12,* 2, 113-127.

Hangartner, J. (1994). *The Constitutionality of Large Scale Police Tactics: Implications for the Right of Intrastate Travel*. School of Law Pace Law Review. [Retrieved from] http://digitalcommons.pace.edu/cgi/viewcontent.cgi?article=1355&context=lawrev

Jones v. North Carolina Prisoners' Labor Union, Inc., 433 U.S. 119 (1977)

Kang, S. (January 01, 2009). Forcing Prison Labor: International Labor Standards, Human Rights and the Privatization of Prison Labor in the Contemporary United States*. *New Political Science, 31,* 2, 137-161.

Kingdon, J. W. (2003). Agendas, alternatives, and public policies. New York: Longman.

National Council on Crime and Delinquency. (2006). Fact sheet: US rates of Incarceration: A global perspective. Washington, DC: Author.

Pelaez, V. (2008). *The prison industry in the United States: big business or a new from of slavery?*. Retrieved from http://www.globalresearch.ca/index.php?context=va&aid=8289

Pew Charitable Trust. (2007). Public safety, public spending: Forecasting America's prison population, 2007-2011. Washington, DC: Author

Ruffin v. Commonwealth, 62 Va. 790, 796 (1871).

Trulson, C. R., & Marquart, J. W. (2009). *First available cell: Desegregation of the Texas prison system*. Austin: University of Texas Press.

U.S. Constitution. 13th Amendment, Sec 1-2.

US Department of Justice. (2001). *Emerging issues on privatized prisons* [Data file]. Retrieved from http://www.ncjrs.gov/pdffiles1/bja/181249.pdf

U.S. General Accounting Office. (1996). Private and public prisons: Studies comparing operational costs and/or quality of services. Washington, DC: Government Printing Office.

Wood, P. J. (January 01, 2007). Globalization and Prison Privatization: Why Are Most of the World's For-Profit Adult Prisons to Be Found in the American South?. *International Political Sociology, 1,* 3, 222-239.

Appendix B

1980's War on Drugs: A Closer Look at Political Agenda and Anti-Drug Legislation

Porscha Kelley

Circa 2010

Introduction

Criminal activity poses a threat to the cohesive and functioning state of society at large. However, the criminalization of activities that do not align with conservative values has long since been used as a mechanism of social control. The demoralization of individuals and the sensationalizing of their criminal act, absent of the full context of their life, allow offenders to be stripped of their constitutional rights and entitlement to objective treatment. When political powers decide they have clout to gain through the exploitation of the perceived deviant behaviors of minority cultures, the constitutional rights of those minorities are easily compromised. The ever-evolving state of the Constitution is used to protect our rights within the growing and maturing matters we face as Americans. However, it is this very same nature that allows politicians and government figureheads to disfigure these pure liberties to their liking. Through this process, the elected-powerful are able to overload the public's psyche and strong-arm America to fit into a conservative box; as this is easily achieved through the enchantment of fear.

For years, our society has looked to federal, state, and local law enforcement agencies to ensure our safety. However, trust and unwavering confidence in the methods and abilities of such agencies has been shaken due to compromising situations and corruption on the part of these same agencies. Specifically, in the late 1980s through the early 1990s, law enforcement in the inner cities focused a tremendous amount of time, energy, and resources on the criminal triad of drugs, guns, and gangs—problems that in combination ignite large spikes in violent crime rates (Hangartner, 1994). During this time, excessive force and new aggressive tactics were used freely with little to no opposition by government officials and overseeing authorities. Despite how appeasing this action may have been to the misinformed public, some critics may categorize these street strategies as scare tactics rather than efficient avenues of problem-solving (Hangartner, 1994).

Several decades have experienced a war on drugs; so many, in fact, that one may question if we are even making any progress. The answer is submerged somewhere under political motives, racial degradation, and a system which purposely underfunds economically and socially sound alternatives in comparisons to punitive sanctions. The 1970's war on drugs, initiated by the Nixon Administration, began in order to garner support among working-class and middle-class whites for Nixon during the election period (Jensen, 1998). This was achieved by "associating cannabis and other illegal drugs with the student left, opponents of the war in Vietnam, and young African-Americans" (Jensen, 1998, p. 13). In combination with the always responsive "get tough on crime" campaign, Nixon increased his following through the argument that drugs and crime are strongly linked. Doing this allowed

225

Nixon's campaign to kill two birds with one stone through the collusion of drugs, crime, and youth/minority self-empowerment movements. This is a classic case of the use of political power in order to pin social problems on targeted "dangerous classes" and to intertwine the "evils" of drugs with the modern social movements to set them back and act as a social barrier (Jensen, 1998, p. 13).

H. R. Haldeman—President Nixon's Chief of Staff—has been quoted in his personal diary to acknowledge that the president "emphasized that you have to face the fact that the whole problem is really the blacks. The key is to devise a system that recognizes this..." (Jensen, 1998, p. 13). This statement alone more than suggests the malicious intentions to distinctly target one set group of individuals based on their race—clearly an unconstitutional act. Nixon and other political leaders have been able to continue this through the creation of a "modern political rhetoric connecting youth, minorities, drugs, and crime," though not particularly in that combination (Jensen, 1998, p 13).

Such political rhetoric in past anti-drug legislation, especially during the 1980s, is aimed at establishing social control and racial/gender disparities. Political actors place personal interests and gains above social welfare, consequently compromising constitutional rights through corruption on the part of government and enforcement officials. An analysis of the affect that political agendas and anti-drug legislation has on federal funds, perceived reputations, and constitutional rights will be reviewed.

Literature Review

Drug use in the U.S., pre-drug war, was diverse, frequent, and facilitated. Around the time of the Civil War, opium was used in patient medicines. Many established businesses that have become staples in American culture found uses of now highly classified drugs. In 1898, the Bayer Corporation made used of heroin as a cough suppressant (Fisher, 2006). Marijuana dates back into early American history; marijuana was "brought to the United States by English settlers and extracts were used by U.S. physicians to produce a tonic for medicinal and recreational purposes" (Fisher, 2006, p. 5). Historical uses of cocaine, absent of negative stigma, in the states dates back to the early 1900s; these uses included the prescription as medical substances or topical anesthetics and even as an ingredient for Coca Cola until it was banned by the Harrison Act (Fisher, 2006; Baum, 1996).

Propaganda Campaign: Opium

Historically, in times of social disorder, diversions are fabricated to deflect attention from the root problem and structured in order to gain political following. Past and present drug campaigns embody the very essence of racial-scapegoating masked by political rhetoric; in this process, racial disparities are consequence, especially through the use of legislation. Early American drug laws are proof of implementation of such campaigns that were staged against immigrants.

In 1875, after the completion of the railroad system, the economy began to slow and the labor market began to decline. Simultaneously, the influx of Chinese immigrants threatened to further degrade the market by providing cheaper labor—specifically within the gold mining and railroad construction industries. Companies active in these two fields were ready to offer significantly lower wages in light of the ample supply of labor in the form of Chinese immigrants who were willing to accept positions without hesitation or negotiation. At this time, Chinese workers, "represented unwanted competition" in an industry with few job opportunities (Jensen, 1998, p. 46). The white labor market answered by taking extreme steps to remove these immigrants from the U.S. labor pool; this campaign was aimed at blameless minorities instead of the "economic power" that held a monopoly over the pricing of the labor market (Jensen, 1998, p. 46).

In order to achieve their goal propaganda campaigns were established to demonize Chinese immigrants, specifically by taking one part of their larger culture, opium, and labeling it as a "subculture of sin" (Jensen, 1998, p. 47). Media assaults persistent in establishing stereotypes were present as early as the late 1890s; in the U.S., films featuring China and the Chinese highlighted opium dens. These images serve to represent "Chinese immigrant[s] who are incapable of resisting imperialism and coercive labor systems" (Marez, 2004, p. 41). Articles were written on the addictive nature of opium, the danger American citizens faced of being "attacked by opium-crazed Chinese offenders," and the risk that respectable citizens could be lured into opium dens (Jensen, 1998, p. 47). Social demonstrations were held and attempts to discontinue immigration from China were fueled absent of any documented evidence of opium use among Chinese immigrants and workers in the United States. Nevertheless, public misinformation and the opportunity to attribute the causation of problems many Americans faced to the Chinese immigrants led to a rallied aversion of that minority group; not too long after this propaganda engendered consensus, this race-based sentiment became evident within the law.

San Francisco, California, was one of the first cities to pass a city ordinance criminalizing the smoking of opium "under penalty of a heavy fine or imprisonment" (Jensen, 1998, p.47). Laws such as this became relatively common among the West Coast. The racially discriminative nature of national drug policy, however, came years later in 1914 with the signing of the Harrison Act. This body of federal legislation "forbade the Chinese living in America to import or manufacture opium that could be smoked in the United States," while allowing only Americans—mostly whites—to import or manufacture opium for the purpose of smoking (Jensen, 1998, p. 47).

Initial restrictions and policies regarding this particular drug were established in order to prevent the spread of an immoral, sinful practice from Chinese immigrants to the citizenry of the U.S. However, years later, the Harrison Act legally allowed white Americans to have dealings in opium; yet banned such activity among Chinese immigrants. One can only argue that such hypocrisy was allowed because the original purpose of the socially constructed opium problem was to create a difference and exclude Chinese laborers from fully participating in the labor market. During the 1950s communist scare, racial-scapegoating again reared its ugly head; the rise in heroin use at the time was attributed to the deceptive efforts of the Chinese. U.S. political leaders coined spawn this occurrence as China's attempt to "overtake the youth of America" and again in the late 1960s complication with youth, "urban civil disorders," and the Vietnam War were diverted through drawing attention to illegal drugs and their users (Jensen, 1998, p. 21). Currently, under the Comprehensive Drug Abuse and Prevention Control Act, opium is listed as a schedule 2 drug. Under this category, drugs are defined as having a high potential for abuse and can lead to psychological or physical dependence (Fisher, 2006).

Propaganda Campaign: Marijuana

The same effort of diversion resulted in a politically constructed campaign against Hispanic immigrants during the early 1900s. The stimulus of anti-Mexican rhetoric in 1930 drug legislation began during the 1930's Great Depression, which harbored a flooded labor pool. Here again, the minority became the scapegoat: a complete diversion for the complete collapse of an entire economic system; the jeopardy of white American job stability; and the threat of immoral criminal activity. Many Americans were "frustrated, bitter, and insecure about their economic future" and accused the Mexican population of taking low-paying jobs from American laborers and being the primary cause of their financial strife (Jensen, 1998, p. 48).

Once again claims-makers extracted a small piece of a minority culture—marijuana use—demonized it and painted it as an epidemic practice. The media aided in the effort of depicting Mexican immigrants "as drug-crazed criminals—made immoral and violent by their use of marijuana" (Jensen, 1998, p. 48). During this time, working-class Mexican men were represented as "threats to law and order in ways that complemented" plans to "police the local supply of 'cheap,' nonunion labor" (Marez, 2004, p. 108). In 1936, the Commissioner of the Bureau of Narcotics, Harry Anslinger, stroked the moral strings of the general public by alleging that a strong relationship existed between marijuana use and criminal behavior including murder, sex crimes, criminal insanity, and other overly violent acts. In order to ensure federal legislation against marijuana use, Anslinger also stated that marijuana had a comparable strength to heroin, insisting that it has a more "socially deleterious" effect than opium, building upon previously constructed stereotypes (Jensen, 1998, p.48).

The marijuana controversy was declared one of the most urgent problems facing the United States. Despite the fact that more than half of the U.S. labor market was out of commission and most banks in the country defaulted, the undocumented use of marijuana prevailed as the most pressing issue of the time amongst lawmakers. Once the real issues were deflected and Anslinger had instilled a fearful hostility among the American people towards Mexican immigrants, President Roosevelt signed the Marijuana Tax Act into law in August 1937. This campaign against Mexican immigrants—used to remove a large portion of them from the labor force—encouraged Americans' bias against not only Mexicans but also most Caribbean populations (Jensen, 1998).

Under the Comprehensive Drug Abuse and Prevention Control Act, marijuana is listed as a schedule 1 drug. Under this category, drugs are defined as having a high potential for abuse, is legally defined as having no accepted medical use in the U.S., and obtains no safe level of use under medical supervision. It is critical to note that marijuana is married to drugs like heroin, LSD, mescaline, peyote, and psilocybin as a schedule 1 substance (Fisher, 2006). Whether marijuana is comparable with these highly addictive drugs is of debate, especial when "there are legal, highly addictive, mind-altering drugs available without prescription in the United States" such as alcohol, caffeine, and nicotine (Fisher, 2006, p. 55).

Introductions of progressive drug use such as cocaine and heroin sparked an even greater campaign that distinctly targeted minorities and women. In a historical review of national drug wars—including the Harrison Act of 1914, the anti-marijuana campaign in the 1930s, the Nixon drug war of the 1970s, and the more aggressive 1980's declaration on the war on drugs, which specifically targeted crack-cocaine—several commonalities arise. Underneath all the rhetorical propaganda we find four main points. First, all drug wars were fueled by state agencies or politicians with some stake in the issue. These problems were constructed and then presented to the public in a sensationalized manner in an attempt to legitimize and solidify the issues at hand (Jensen, 1998). Second, the underlying, yet readily apparent, "institutional racism" is exhibited in both the judicial and criminal justice system, as reflected in the mandatory sentencing disparity between crack and powder cocaine (Jensen, 1998, p. 21). Third, societal problems were attributed to illegal drugs (Jensen, 1998). Lastly, the media exacerbated the situation by "recreating worst cases into typical cases and the episodic into the epidemic" (Jensen, 1998, p. 21).

Political Agendas

The 1980's War on Drugs and events leading up to are associated with the struggle for political clout. The golden rule of politics during election season is to exploit "public predispositions" based more on the majority's prejudice or preference than on policy making (Jensen, 1998, p. 17); this is a basic tactic used when gaining and/or retaining a political position. During almost any election period, crime control comes to the forefront of all political platforms.

A plethora of bills and new programs are paraded, promises on crime eradication are made, and appearances coupled with speeches are seen in the media. In 1973, Congress quickly passed Nixon's plan to field a new agency under the Justice Department; the Office of Drug Abuse Law Enforcement (ODALE) and Bureau of Narcotics and Dangerous Drugs (BNDD) combined to form the Drug Enforcement Administration (DEA), whose "primary [original] mission" would be to intercept the *highest* levels of illicit drug traffic and avoid street-level pushers (Baum, 1996, p. 86). During the 1980s, bills were introduced by both the Democratic and Republican Parties, which resorted in one of the biggest drug policies—the $1.7 billion Drug-Free America Act (Jensen, 1998). Outrageous goals went unchecked during this time in the enthusiasm of bill writing; the 1988 Anti-Drug Abuse Act was governed with the purpose to "create a Drug-Free America by 1995"—an impossible feat (Sterling, 2004, p. 62).

In 1988, the Office of National Drug Control Policy (ONDCP) was established under the Reagan Administration; this office was under direct instruction to "prevent young people from using illicit drugs, reduce the number of people using illicit drugs, and decrease the availability of illicit drugs" (Fisher, 2006, p. 5). Additionally, strong anti-drug legislative acts set the stage for political control to be expressed through enforcement tactics. By the time George H. Bush left office, the Fourth Amendment (search and seizure), Fifth Amendment (protection from abuse of government authority in legal procedure), Sixth Amendment (speedy trial, counsel, and right to an impartial jury), and Eight Amendment (cruel and unusual punishment) Amendments had been greatly suppressed within many criminal justice agencies' operations (Jensen, 1998, p. 54). Through this suppression, protection barriers against unconstitutional measures and tyrannical abuses of authority dissipated; consequently, the most aggressive war on drugs evolved (Baggins, 1998, p. 55). The subject of drugs had totally consumed the political prospective; the proceeding years were full of presidential candidates accusing the other of being "soft on drugs," so much so that "political actors" acknowledged how "everybody wants to out-drug each other in terms of political rhetoric" (Jensen, 1998, p. 19).

Traditional politicians were not the only individuals jumping on the "drug bandwagon" in order to better their following and reputation. In an attempt to appeal to the public, First Lady Nancy Reagan, known for being unaware and detached from mainstream America, endorsed the drug issue and the fight to clean up the streets. Nancy Regan appeared on the poplar 1980s ABC sitcom *Diff'rent Strokes* to "promote her infamous answer to the drug problem—'Just say no'" (Marez, 2004, p. 1). In a 1989, crack-house raid, led by Los Angeles Police Department (LAPD) Chief Darryl Gates, Nancy Reagan made a "photo op," appearing in a LAPD windbreaker. As the Special Weapons and Tactics team pulled several black teenagers from the house, Nancy Reagan pronounced that "these people in here are beyond the point of teaching and rehabilitation" (Baggins, 1998, p. 135).

By the end of 1986, crack had hit many major eastern cities in the U.S., and many notable politicians had successfully championed the drug problem. As a result, public awareness of the issue had risen; many acknowledged drugs to be the most urgent problem for the nation. One of the most resounding themes of the 1980's war on drugs is anti-drug policy and its criminalization of deviant behavior in order to control or suppress it. These policies often leave room for constitutional rights to be compromised as they present barriers to this process (Baggins, 1998, p. 55).

The collusion of several branches of government and political leaders—this includes judicial, executive, and enforcement officials—occurs on a large scale. Near the end of the 1980s, Chief Justice Rehnquist aided in the abridging of constitutional rights when he announced that the judiciary's job in the war on drugs was to secure the prosecution and incarceration of a throng of Americans (Baggins, 1998, p. 55). Rehnquist even beseeched Congress to create several new district courts in order to sustain "conviction productivity," in anticipation of the federal bench falling behind on drug cases (Baggins, 1998, p. 55). The very disdain expressed through these sentiments of judicial responsibility makes it readily translucent that judicial actors, particularly in drug cases, were steadfastly looking to convict at all costs, turning a blind eye to unconstitutional actions on the part of police or any other criminal justice agencies.

Anti-drug legislation as a whole has the ostensive goal of bettering society by maintaining social order, reducing the number of drug-related health problems, and minimizing "the immorality associated with drug use" (Jensen, 1998, p. 45). However, many critics have found that drug policies are more concerned with street-drug distributors than with drug smugglers and sources. Drug laws have been used as "institutionalized mechanisms by which the socially powerful pursue their own political and economic interests" (Jensen, 1998, p. 45). Such criticism is sustained when the punitive nature of drug laws are examined—including racially disproportionate incarceration levels and more retributive rather than rehabilitative consequences.

Institutionalizing Racial Disparity

The use of crack, especially in poor urban areas inhabited by minorities, diverted attention from bigger social and economic issues during the 1980s; politicians were ultimately able to blame a "powerless group for social disaster" (Jensen, 1998, p. 54). This became very easy to do once "crack was perceived as the drug of choice for the dangerous black underclass" and Congress came to the unanimous decision that crack cocaine was more dangerous than powder cocaine (Jensen, 1998, p. 54). The passing of federal drug laws resulted in mandatory sentencing; specifically, the federal penalty of a five year sentence for possession of five or more grams of crack-cocaine. However, bias in this law is readily apparent when compared to the penalty for possessing the same amount of powder-cocaine; if a person is caught in possession of powder-cocaine, then they would have to have at least 500 grams or more in order to receive the same five-year sentence. This has been distinguished as the "hundred-to-one rule," which has continued to ensure a disparity in sentencing, especially among racial lines (Jensen, 1998, p. 50).

Mandatory sentencing laws, for those charged with possession and/or drug trafficking, were enacted by Congress and states followed with similar penalties; this directly affected state prison admissions on a large scale. Sentencing policies of the 1980s and 1990s decreased judicial discretion and brought about longer mandatory minimum sentences (Bosworth & Flavin, 2007). The amount of drug-related offenders imprisoned increased by 231% between the years 1981-1992. In 1992, state prison admissions averaged 61% for drug offenses alone (Jensen, 1998). As a result, by the mid 1990s, one out of every four state inmates was incarcerated because of a non-violent drug offense (Piche et al., 2002, p. 197). Sentencing under anti-drug law is haphazardly unbalanced where the punishment far outweighs a non-violent crime.

In New York State, the possession or sale of one or two ounces, respectively, results in a mandatory minimum prison sentence of fifteen years and paroled lifetime supervision therefore after (Sterling, 2004). This seems utterly ridiculous when the Department of Justice (DOJ) reports that offenders of harsher violations like rape—in which another person is victimized—was sentenced to an average of 117 months (or 9.75 years) in prison in the year of 1992; of this sentence, the actual time served in prison averaged 65 months (or 5.4 years). In 1986, the maximum penalty for violating the Federal Controlled Substances Act of 1970 was raised by Congress from 20 years to the chance of receiving a life sentence (Sterling, 2004). Perhaps intuitive in the act of inflating the serious offender pool, the consequence of the many woes our criminal justice system faces today, including: swamped criminal court dockets, further subjugation of minorities, over-crowded prisons, and the inability to finance such a system.

The growing drug arrests resulting from 1980s' drug policies—and the overzealous willingness to incarcerate non-violent drug offenders—are seen as the "most likely culprits for the current racial disparity in our nation's prison" (Pratt, 2009, p. 7). These federal drug laws, specifically those implementing mandatory sentencing, were "in theory applied in a discriminatory fashion against minorities" (Jensen, 1998, p. 55). Disparities among racial arrest-rates are said to be attributed largely to the hundred-to-one rule in which "African-Americans were much more likely than other races to be arrested for distributing small amounts of crack cocaine" (Fisher, 2006, p. 5).

The U.S. Department of Justice cited that from the years 1980 to 1994 the number of African-American males incarcerated throughout the nation increased by 225% (Jensen, 1998); during this same time span (1980-1994), Bureau of Justice Statistics indicated that African-Americans were incarcerated at a rate of seven times more than whites. During 1986-1991, arrest rates for minority-juvenile drug offenders increased 78% while the arrest rate of white juvenile drug offenders decreased by 34% (Piche et al., 2002, p. 202).This results almost solely from the popular strategy where "police tend to target minority group neighborhoods in the pursuit of drug law violators, while leaving middle-class white neighborhoods virtually untouched (Jensen, 1998, p. 55).

In the early 1990s, despite a seemingly cohesive political backing of tight drug crackdowns, opposition regarding such subjective laws emitted from law-conscious individuals. In 1993, the Chief Judge of the U.S. District Court in Nebraska sentenced four African-American crack cocaine dealers to serve a substantially shorter period than that mandated by federal statutes. The judge reasoned his decision based on the observation that African-Americans were "being treated unfairly in receiving substantially longer sentences than Caucasian males who traditionally deal in powder cocaine" (Jensen, 1998, p. 52). This ruling was subsequently overturned in a higher court, citing "...that even if the guidelines are unfair to African-Americans, [it] is not enough to justify a more lenient sentence than called for under the [federal] guidelines" (Jensen, 1998, p. 52).

In 1991, estimates from the National Institute on Drug Abuse (NIDA) reported that crack cocaine users were distributed in the following manner: 50% were white, 36% were African-American, and 14% were Hispanic (Jensen, 1998, p. 50). Conversely, a 1995 estimate reported that of those convicted of crack cocaine, charges were distributed in the following manner: 93% were African-American, 5% were white, and 3% were Hispanic (Jensen, 1998, p. 50). Currently, for the past 20 years, "drug use rates among black youths have been consistently lower per capita" than that of white youths (Piche et al., 2002, p. 189).The U.S. Department of Justice reported that in 1993, whites convicted of a federal drug offense served an average of 74 months in prison, while African-Americans served a term averaging 98 months (Jensen, 1998). Sentencing disparities were highlighted by racially discriminative undertones present in political rhetoric at the time. If the goal of the 1980's war on drugs was to make a bold attempt to clear a large majority of crack off the streets, then it would make more sense to go after the largest percentage of users in order to achieve such a goal.

The divide on this issue seems to rest on the racially fostered mythology that "cocaine is Hollywood, crack is Harlem" (Jensen, 1998, p. 53). Historically, in almost all areas where race is directly or indirectly involved, equality invariably threatens the interests of the powerful. In the case of the hundred-to-one rule, federal appellate courts have cited that federal drug guidelines do not violate the Fourteenth Amendment's Equal Protection Clause, even though overtly contrary observations exist (Jensen, 1998).

In efforts to close the disparity in punishment regarding power versus crack, the Sentencing Commission—responsible for the development, collection, and analysis of federal policy and sentencing issues—proposed amending federal guidelines (Graciana et al, 2010). On three different occasions their recommendation to balance prosecution sentences among these two substances were dismissed by Congress. The Sentencing Commission's first proposal, in 1995, attempted to set the five year mandatory sentencing minimum at a 1-to-1 ratio (Graciana et al, 2010). Their second attempt, in 1997, pushed for a 10-to-1 ratio (Graciana et al, 2010). Their final attempt in appealing to Congress and the president, in 2002, conservatively advocated a 20-to-1 ratio (Graciana et al, 2010).

Many argue that such consequences of institutional laws, like the hundred-to-one rule, are established to maintain the status quo and sustain minorities as the underclass. This argument is bolstered by the persistence that numerous collections of experiments and research have yielded similar conclusions that additional surveillance, more severe penalties, and mandatory sentences do not substantially reduce crime. Nevertheless, these same tactics were the very same used during the 1980's War on Drugs, consequently resulting in the incarceration of a disproportionate amount of minorities. Inclusive in this population were females, specifically minority females.

As a direct consequence of stricter anti-drug enforcement, the 1990s produced a disparity in drug-related arrests among men and women (Bosworth & Flavin, 2007). Within the criminal justice system, a pronounced increase of arrest rates for women charged with drug-related offenses occurred. Near the conclusion of the 1990s, one in three state female prisoners was serving drug-related sentences (Bosworth & Flavin, 2007). Specifically in New York, during 1996, sixty percent of those women imprisoned were sentenced for a drug offense while only thirty-two percent of all men imprisoned at the time were sentenced under drug charges (Bosworth & Flavin, 2007, p. 186).

Such a distribution could possibly be explained away by the general understanding that men commit a wider range of crime. However, a 1994 Department of Justice study showed that even within the same category of crime—drug-related offenses—women sentenced to federal prison for low-level offenses were subjected to sentences equivalent to men sentenced to federal prison for more serious drug offenses. Furthermore, within female arrests, Latinas and African American woman were more likely to be arrested for drug offenses than white women. The percentage of arrest-rates for female minorities was inequitably distributed in comparison to their racial makeup population-wise. For example, Coramae Mann's 1990 Study in New York found that Latinas made up only 28% of women *arrested* for a drug offense but were 42% of the women who were *convicted* and imprisoned for such offenses (Bosworth & Flavin, 2007, p. 186).

The situation seems simple: if you punish one citizen for committing a crime against society, then it is only just to punish another in the same manner for committing a fairly equated crime. In this instance, it is apparent that it was not necessarily the type of cocaine that warrants the punitive repercussions but the person in possession of the drug. When this type of practice is condoned, the general principle of a punishment deserving of the crime is disregarded and diminished; blind judgments are made which can vary widely and distort the entire reasoning for condemning the offender.

Politically Financial

The constructed campaign for the war on drugs is directly affiliated with urban crime and violence; these attributes designated this campaign as an underclass problem and made it easier for Republican-led assaults on welfare and affirmative action to persist (Jensen, 1998). Diversions from social issues such as homelessness, unemployment, and educational inequalities allowed federal resources to be spent irresponsibly. Politicians, officials, and enforcement representatives used the drug issue to their advantage, both financially and policy-wise.

Ill-focused street tactics to destroy the drug market through the enforcement of more punitive laws may have actually increased the attractiveness of selling illegal drugs. The criminalization of crack-cocaine increased street prices and resulted in large-scale dealers making large-scale profits with many incentives to expand their market (Jensen, 1998). An enormous amount of financial resources were squandered by federal office holders; at the highest level of distribution, profits from drug sales trumped the threat of incarceration. For drug agencies, the task of dissipating a crack-cocaine customer base of millions was an insurmountable task, especially with a lack of rehabilitative funding. Some criminology scholars popularly speculate that federal drug laws are not even structured in a way that promotes achieving such a goal. These laws may in fact perpetuate political interests and the art of passing the buck.

In 1994, Justice Research under the National Criminal Justice Association reported estimates which indicated that to reduce cocaine use by 1% through drug treatment would require an additional thirty-four million dollars. Conversely, to achieve the same feat through domestic enforcement would require an additional one billion dollars; the 1980's war on drugs and anti-drug legislation obviously rested on the "incitement of fear" and a tremendous effort to emphasize punishment because resources were allocated to the latter tactic (Jensen, 1998, pg. 56). Despite the billions of dollars thrown at the "most aggressive drug war campaign in history," the amount of cocaine smuggled into the U.S. during the year 1987 increased to 35,970 kilograms in comparison to the 1,872 kilograms smuggled in 1981 (Jensen, 1998, p. 50). This surplus of cocaine had actually reduced its price by one-third and made crack and cocaine products easier to buy on the street than marijuana, further exacerbating the distribution of drugs.

The underlying motive of the expansion of the socially constructed war on drugs was money. In efforts to gain a cut of anti-drug federal funds, law enforcement agencies openly invited journalists to ride-alongs of drug busts, offered in-depth interviews, and issued numerous press releases in order to fuel the fire and "to promote journalistic attention to drugs" (Jensen, 1998, p. 35). As a result, federal spending on drug enforcement increased an estimated ten billion dollars between the years 1981 and 1993 (Jensen, 1998). Ironically, this victory in financial growth for law enforcement decreased the funds available for drug treatment/prevention. At this point, the federal government did not attempt to eradicate cocaine's existence on the street through rehab and education, but rather by force. Therefore, overall, "the modern drug war, during the

Reagan-Bush Administrations, [cost] the taxpayer in excess of $150 billion" (Baggins, 1998, p. 127).

Media

Throughout the 1980's, public opinion polls overseen by the Gallup Organization revealed that the public was generally unconcerned about illicit drugs. Once President Ronald Reagan announced his attack on drugs in August of 1986, the media focused on drug coverage, specifically focused on crack-cocaine. The media had great influence in shaping the drug scare. Print media were criticized for distorting research findings in order to paint a picture of "a coke plague" (Jensen, 1998, p.17). TV media venues were cited as providing as many as seventy-four evening news segments on drugs in July of 1986 alone; during this same year, "48 Hours on Crack Street" received the highest Neilson rating of a news show in the previous five years (Jensen, 1998, p.17).

For enforcement and policy-shaping purposes the public were cajoled into believing that street gangs predominately drove drug sales. Research, however, has established that "inner-city street gangs do not have exclusive control over crack distribution" (Jacobs, 1999, p. 10). Although the selling of crack and gang membership correlate one cannot be said to be the causation of the other. Many street distributors are not gang members, however, "gangs provide the connections and criminal capital necessary to do business" (Jacobs, 1999, p. 10). News coverage of the drug issue in the 1980's increased the public's awareness and concern, directly influencing the percentage of Americans who polled drugs as the number-one problem facing the country. Drug rhetoric and a growing public awareness legitimized punitive drug policies. Public opinion is and has always been an intricate and multifaceted collection of ideas; through polls and surveys these complex perceptions are watered down and interpreted at face value by politicians. Consequently, the 1980's drug news coverage "encouraged people to identify law enforcement as the appropriate solution to this complex social problem" (Jensen, 1998, p. 36).

Print and television media venues endorsed "the right-wing view that punishment of urban minority sin was the focal domestic agenda" (Baggins, 1998, p. 135). The media's primary contribution to the war on drugs was their manipulation of white cocaine users and black crack users through the discrepancy in coverage, ultimately impacting the public's opinion (Baggins, 1998). In the years in which cocaine use was defined as a "recreational drug"— particularly by the "prosperous white" culture—contextual storytelling based on the user warranted a medicinal model for treatment (Baggins, 1998, p. 134). However, 1980's media coverage of watered down crack-cocaine, quickly defined by its urban black users, set out "to raise the alarm of the enemy within"—more clearly identified as the poor subculture (Baggins, 1998, p. 135).

Sterling (2004) argues that drug policy contradicts of a restorative policy, especially with respect to the drug user, who is then punished for addiction, a sickness. In addition to the dissonance of discretion on the part of judges (in part by mandatory sentencing), the movement from a treatment-perspective to a punitive-perspective, especially in the portrayal of addicts, has dissected the offenders from wider society and further made it easier to build an "empathic divide" and then subject them to excessive punishment (Haney, 2005, p. 203).

Corruption

With constitutionally stripped, politically driven tactics used in the fight against drugs, street-level actors in the 1980's war on drugs may have easily fallen prey to personal pursuits of financial gains. Corruption at both state and federal levels persists in environments in which Constitutional procedures are discarded (Baggins, 1998). The Federal Bureau of Investigation (FBI), the Drug Enforcement Agency (DEA), and the Central Intelligence Agency (CIA) have all had a substantial amount of evidence brought against them alleging they have been corrupted by drug prohibition. The year 1996 stood as the year of exposure; deception and high profile malfeasance was brought to light. In this very year, the FBI's crime labs' "scientific" conclusions were found to have rested on falsified reports in order to "prove" an agent's suspicion for court purposes (Baggins, 1998, p. 15). Additionally, major actors of the DEA—in a more criminal versus procedural disregard—were suspected of profiting directly from funds and resources made available to their agency. In 1996, DEA Supervising Agent Clifford Shibata was indicted on thirteen counts of embezzlement. In his defense, he asserted that the agency had "sloppy record keeping" in terms of money and drugs used in drug buys—insinuating that no one could possibly decipher what has been taken, who has taken it, and how much they have taken (Baggins, 1998, p. 15).

Holistically, it seems highly hypocritical that presidential administrations hell-bent on enforcing the social reform of the anti-drug campaign are wrought in drug-affiliated controversy. Marez (2004) draws on historical affiliations that have surfaced over time; for instance, the Nixon Administration had ties to "Southeast Asian heroin traffic in order to fund the War in Vietnam" (Marez, 2004, p. 1). Additionally, the Regan Administration lent support to the " Cocaine Coup," a military takeover funded by drug barons; Manuel Noriega's Panamanian dictatorship—a ruling that was rancid with the laundering of drug money; and the cocaine trade in the

U.S., used to "fund the contra's attack on the Nicaraguan Revolution" (Marez, 2004, p.2).

A certain level of corruption and misconduct is an unavoidable occurrence in large organizations; even officers fall victim to the loss of integrity and legitimacy when such shortcomings are evident. In particular, studies conducted, in reference to the LAPD, argue that misconduct within this department existed through four distinctive themes (Baggins, 1998). First was the "growing sense by police that the public is the enemy" (Baggins, 1998, p.6); this distorted cultured ideology placed the first divider between the LAPD and those individuals they were to serve and protect. Here, leadership philosophy permeated and played a huge part in how officers interacted with the public. Secondly, the "substitution of the mission of police work from public safety to cultural control" set the stage for corrupt action to take place, even if it superseded written law or moral consciousness (Baggins, 1998, p. 6). Thirdly, a "loss of respect for the public in the communities targeted for control" formed and the "hostility" expressed towards the residents of the Los Angeles community which was then reciprocated (Baggins, 1998, p. 7). The cycle of animosity between the community and police persisted throughout the 1980s. Last, the police developed a capacity to affirm and legitimize a "disregard of constitutional promises and citizen rights" (Baggins, 1998, p. 6). Once Americans' rights become barriers for "coercive government authority" to achieve "cultural control," such rights are restricted, as history accounts (Baggins, 1998, p. 6).

Due to these issues, within the LAPD there existed an environment prone to chaos, complete with "weak civilian oversight," officers that harbored distrust of management, low morale, and a "dysfunctional partnership with community members" (Grant, 2003, p. 392).

Eventually, misconduct was solidified once LAPD officers realized their attempt to clean crack completely off the streets through excessively coercive methods was futile; officers easily succumbed to alluring profits of the underworld drug game (Baggins, 1998). Although some forms of corruption were achieved at the street-level, most specialized police units could not have taken part in large-scale corruption and scandal without "collusion on the parts of district attorneys, judges, and top law-enforcement officials" (Grant, 2003, p. 387). Misconduct cover-ups were readily available considering Justice Rehnquist's insistence that the judiciary be willing to convict and overly prosecute in the War on Drugs.

The Crossing of Constitutional Boundaries

The LAPD's response to increasing crime rates and extreme gang-related activity during the 1980s involved heightened "aggressive tactics rather than progressive community policing" (Hangartner, 1994, p. 208). This choice in strategy further exacerbated the disconnection between officers and residents; utilizing "automobile-based preventive patrol," where the main focus was on keeping all units "in-service," had officers in patrol cars cruising Los Angeles at all times. In essence, this marginalized officers' association with members of the community, leading to conditions that further bred the "us versus them" attitude (Prenzler, 2009, p. 24). The LAPD developed and sustained a long-standing reputation for their use of intimidation and pervasive presence, a stigma further cultivated through the leadership at the time. Such use of excessive force in combination with racial profiling, especially within non-violent situations, resulted in "a lopsided number of blacks being arrested for nonviolent drug crime" (Piche et al., 2002, p. 187); consequently, notable accounts of incidents concluded in lawsuits fought and settled against the LAPD such as the $15 million settlement received by Javier Ovando and the $3.8 million settlement received by Rodney King.

Specifically, during the time period of 1978 to 1992, LAPD chief Darryl Gates, through his actions and choice of words, set the tone for the police force and what attitude they would take *protecting* the streets of Los Angeles. Herbert (1996) has emphasized that the overly aggressive policing for which the LAPD is notorious bred "tremendous distrust between the police and the citizenry" (52). Gates boldly showcased his internal morals while making a comment to the U.S. Senate Committee that, in his opinion, even casual drug users deserved to be taken out and shot (Hangartner, 1994). A loss of respect for Gates and the LAPD among the public within the Los Angeles area was solidified by several racist comments made by Gates during his career. Therefore, African Americans in the Los Angeles area became more suspicious of the police than the drug dealers on the street ("NWA: The World's Most Dangerous Group," 2008). This suspicion was justified by the fact that three-quarters of young black men in the Los Angeles area were being arrested by the LAPD at the time (Baggins, 1998).

Furthermore, Gates internalized the "show-of-force strategy," substituting public safety for cultural control as evident in the 1988 "Operation Hammer" initiative. In response to the massive increase in gang-related crime, including drug sales, a 160-officer anti-gang unit was assembled to target specific communities and perform nightly "sweeps" (Hangartner, 1994, p. 211). These sweeps were accompanied by field investigations during which officers searched a large number of Los Angeles residents who fit the "gang profile" according to race, age, and style of dress. These investigations resulted in the questioning of over 2,400 people a week (Hangartner, 1994). Reportedly, the series of questioning consisted of officers stopping an individual or group and filling out cards with the person's name, alias, and a list of that person's associates. However, more candid video interviews with residents within these particular neighborhoods portray very different accounts of the situation. Several individuals testified that these sweeps usually resulted in further harassment, verbal abuse, and often concluded by the person being "taken for a ride," which consisted of being forced into a patrol car, beaten, and then thrown behind a building out of sight ("NWA: The World's Most Dangerous Group," 2008).

LAPD started using the "sweeps" tactic in the mid 1980s, primarily on weekend nights—while "general social activity and gang activity" was at its peak (Hangartner, 1994, p. 200). While these sweeps ostensibly controlled gang activity and associated violence, they were not performed in "'an effort to take a lot of drugs off the street,' but rather to 'take people off the street'"—under the reign of Chief Gates (qtd. In Hangartner, 1994, p. 204). In efforts to extend social control and further restrict constitutional safeguards, LAPD sweeps actually "act[ed] as a de facto curfew" (Hangartner, 1994, p. 204). During the hours of such operations, the police discouraged and prevented a large portion of residents in minority-saturated communities from leaving their homes as they would normally do so, consequently impeding on the "constitutional rights of assembly and association" (Hangartner, 1994, p. 204).

The right of association is implied in the First Amendment right to assembly and the Supreme Court has subsequently recognized it to be "a necessary corollary" (Hangartner, 1994, p. 212). When law-abiding citizens are largely inconvenienced by those whose job it is to *serve and protect*, the goals, vision, and mechanics of performing police work are skewed in a dangerous and misguided fashion. In essence, the LAPD became unbalanced and acted like more of a bother than the drug dealers who terrorized the streets.

Special Unit Discretion

The LAPD was among the first local police departments to invest in specialized units, Special Weapons and Tactics (SWAT) being the most imitated. During the 1980s war on drugs, Chief Gates approved the formation of Community Resources Against Street Hoodlums (CRASH); this unit was one of the most aggressive and invasive units on the streets during the 1980s. Because drug use cases are rarely ever coupled with a "victim" who files a complaint, the argument for more proactive tactics may have some substantive ground. However, with the rapid evolution of drug laws and the criminalization of drug use, there existed an intense pressure to "extend the intrusiveness of [agents'] techniques for enforcing drug laws" (Jensen, 1998, p. 22). This extension perhaps expanded those techniques far beyond the span of constitutional safeguards. Ultimately, these specialized units offered limited coordinated information, were unmanaged (self-managed), and "out of institutional control and unaccountable" (Punch, 2009, p. 243).

Methods employed by members of LAPD's subunits personified the "by any means necessary" attitude, ignoring procedural conduct and the preservation of citizens' rights. The LAPD unquestioningly gave the CRASH unit "wide latitude" in their ability to enforce "street justice" (Grant, 2003, p. 392). This wide discretion was influenced and furthermore condoned by top-level leadership, among whom scandal and injustice were carried out. The free-reign allotted to special units within the LAPD also allowed for the misappropriation of services, so much so that the unit cultivated standard cover-up procedures where "a code was sent out over a private frequency, and sentries [guarded] the door while unit members met to discuss strategy" (Grant, 2003, p. 392).

The Rampart division of the LAPD, like CRASH, made routine use of brutality and imitation; in particular, this division used the Department of Immigration and Naturalization to compile a list of deportable Hispanics to act as unwilling respondents in the surveillance of drug activity within the community (Piche et al., 2002, p. 191). In spite of the lack of eye-witness cooperation—in part due to the aggressive tactics used by police and their tarnished relationship within the community—specialized units were initially very successful in obtaining convictions within the courtroom (Herbert, 1996). Consequently, however, many of these convictions were overturned due to the exposure of procedural misconduct of these same specialized units. Rafael Perez, a snitch in the Rampart scandal, admitted to hundreds of accounts of perjury in search of false convictions, false arrest and fabrications of evidence (Gross, et al., 2005). A "structural view" of such specialized units indicates that CRASH and Rampart were not anomalies of the LAPD, and, on a larger scale, represented a resounding pattern within the criminal justice system (Grant, 2003, p. 392).

When scandals surface, it is easy to blame a few "rotten apples" within a police department, but when numerous scandals invade hierarchical tiers, the public is forced to take a second look at policing within that community and perhaps throughout America. Through historical review, there is ample evidence that suggests "Los Angeles offers a microcosm of the general tragedy of criminal justice" (Baggins, 1998, p. 9). A clear view lends "a structural tension between force and law that further results in a tendency for police to repeatedly use power inappropriately" (Grant, 2003, p. 386).

On a broader scale, the use of enforcement, absent of education and treatment models, has been argued to have the underlying motive to use drug trafficking as a reason to further expand military power (Marez, 2004). After Regan's 1986 declaration of the danger drug trafficking posed to the U.S., the boundaries instituted by the Posse Comitatus Act—requiring federal uniformed services from exercising state law enforcement powers to maintain law and order—were succinctly dissipated. This was readily apparent in the integration of "local, state, and federal police forces" and the use of "military training, intelligence, and hardware with domestic police powers" (Marez, 2004, p. 4-5). This was seen in the use of helicopters, heightened high-tech surveillance techniques, tanks (otherwise known as the battle-ram in the LAPD "Operation Hammer"), and raids.

Discussion

Historically, members of society have retaliated when unconstitutional safeguards are crossed, most notably seen in social upraises and riots. Time, attitudes, and generational changes slowly erode previous ideologies based on propaganda and generalizations instituted through sensationalized political coverage. Even though the dominant culture makes bold attempts to control what is morally accepted and what will be criminally punished, the will of wider society eventually proves significant. Social control can be strained by the ever-evolving variable social change.

Pending Legalization of Marijuana

In recent events, Americans see this occurring in the state of California in the fight to legalize the privatization of growth and distribution of marijuana. Such an act has been frowned upon for years, but as politicians and economists find promise in the taxing of such sales, settling a tapped state-budget seems to trump the moral obligations of many political leaders. A proposition to legalize marijuana was placed on the November 2010 ballot ("Bid to Put Tax on Pot Makes Ballot," 2010). Within this proposition, the Regulate, Control, and Tax Cannabis Act "would authorize the cultivation, transport and sale of marijuana" which would then be taxed ("Bid to Put Tax on Pot Makes Ballot," 2010). An endorsing statement made by Governor Arnold Schwarzenegger, Republican, "gave credence to [the] potential revenue source [which] the state's tax chief said could raise $ 1.3 billion [during] the recession" ("Support for Legalizing Marijuana Grows Rapidly around U.S," 2009). An October 2009 Gallup Poll found that 44% of Americans would be in favor of legalizing marijuana ("Support for Legalizing Marijuana Grows Rapidly around U.S," 2009); in this case it is unclear whether political endorsement followed public opinion or vice versa.

Recreational use of cannabis, over several decades, has lost those strongly held "implications of social protest and opposition" it once carried in the mainstream public (Shiner, 2009, p. 163). Collectively, the punitive nature of drug policy in the U.S., spanning the last four decades, has attempted to "legislat[e] out" the existence of consumer demand; this choice of tactic has consequently "left [Americans] with a drug problem worse than that of any other wealthy nation" (Shiner, 2009, p. 167).

Rethinking Enforcement Tactics

In light of current shifts in social change, as seen in recent state and federal disjuncture concerning marijuana, the tri-fold debate of legalization versus decriminalization versus harm reduction has intensified. Legalization calls for the changing of laws to allow for the legal possession and/or distribution of a substance; an example would include the legalization of substances for medicinal purposes only. Decriminalization occurs when a drug user is not charged with a crime depending on the "amount of the drug in the possession of the person or the circumstances in which it is being used" (Fisher, 2006, p. 55). Harm reduction is a policy that recognizes that illicit drug use cannot be eliminated and focus on assisting drug use in the safest manner possible; implications in such a policy can be seen in needle exchange programs (Fisher, 2006).

The understanding between state and federal government is in conflict, perhaps exhibiting a great disconnect amid actions of social control and the will of free society, where some states have made it legal for the possession and use of medical marijuana, "the federal government has maintained that federal laws prohibiting the possession or use of marijuana supersede state laws" (Fisher, 2006, p. 54). Such conflict begs the question if other illicit substances will follow in the controversy of re-categorizing drug schedules and uses, especially in the wake of the exponential growth of the American prison system due to strict anti-drug legislation.

On May 1, 2007, the Sentencing Commission applied amendments to federal guidelines regarding crack offenses, subsequently reducing the amount of time sentenced for possession of five or more grams (Graciana et al., 2010). On March 3, 2008, the retroactive component of the amendment became effective allowing those offenders sentenced before November 1, 2007, who met eligibility requirements, to apply for a sentence reduction (Graciana et al., 2010). In July 2008, the Sentencing Commission issued a preliminary report showing that only "for months after the retroactive amendment went into effect, 7,513 offenders had been granted sentence reductions" (Graciana et al., 2010, p. 16). This warranted leniency will no doubt ease the budgetary burdens of prisons across the country experiencing over-crowding.

Conclusion

The war on drugs—whether the decade denotes a special focus on opium, marijuana, cocaine, or any other criminalized substance—is one of a vague nature. The word "war" has a military undertone which implies a struggle between "good guys" and "bad guys" (Fisher, 2006, p. 162); in the sense that the tag line "War on Drugs" is used throughout political rhetoric, no "bad guy" is specified. Is the target of this war the drugs, drug dealers, drug distributors, the drug users, or all of the above? Technically speaking, the end results of any effort can never be measured if there are no quantifiable criteria of what constitutes achievement. If a drug-free America is the criteria, then it is safe to say that efforts of the 1980's struggle for a 'drug free' America were futile at the expense of billions of tax dollars tied up in enforcement tactics and the thousands of non-violent drug offenders sent to prison.

The paradox of the declaration on the war on drugs of the 1980's was the fact that drug use—according to self-reported status of use—for a majority of most age groups peaked during the 1970s and remained sustainably stable during the 1980's. An even more comprehensive study conducted by the National Institute on Drug Abuse surveyed drug use and recorded an overall peak in use between the years of 1979 through 1982 then remained steady, except for cocaine which rose dramatically during 1982-1985 (Jensen, 1998, p. 14). Crack-cocaine arrived on the streets around this very time giving politicians a reason to jump on the 'tough on crime' bandwagon. Speeches were made and anti-drug legislation was dished out to satisfy citizenry at the costs of tactical reasoning and treatment.

One thing is certain, that our current and past approach" has been ineffective in reducing drug use, saving, lives, reducing crime, or hindering drug traffickers" (Sterling, 2004, p. 54). In many ways our drug war mirrors the prohibition of alcohol through possibly increasing its popularity and therefore crime. As a means of social control, "…prohibition is an ineffective and counterproductive form of control, which forfeits the possibility of effective regulation by pushing drug use into illicit markets" (Shiner, 2009, p. 168).

Money, power, and respect resonate as the underlying themes of the long fight in the war on drugs. The resurgence of battles—masked by enemy sub-cultures and propaganda inflated demonizing—waged during political shifts in power, are based unequivocally more on personal interests than the well-being of society as a whole. It appears that in politicians' ability to easily distract the public from substantial and deeply rooted issues, we keep fighting a "war" with bullets, racially biased diversions, and compounded laws when the answers are buried under education, opportunity, and rehabilitation. We will never 'win' a fixed battle, especially when the war being fought is wrought with political and economic agendas. Excessive punitive measures does not make much of a difference when dealers are replaced instantly, which implies that the problem is deeper than enforcement.

Reference

Baggins, D. S. (1998). *Drug hate and the corruption of American justice*. Westport, Conn: Praeger.

Baum, D. (1996). *Smoke and mirrors: The war on drugs and the politics of failure*. Boston: Little, Brown.

Bosworth, M., & Flavin, J. (2007). *Race, gender, and punishment: From colonialism to the war on terror*. Critical Issues In Crime and Society. New Brunswick, N.J.: Rutgers University Press.

Fisher, G. L. (2006). *Rethinking our war on drugs: Candid talk about controversial issues*. Westport, Conn: Praeger.

Graciana, K., Blackburn, A., Fowler, S. (2010) Federal Crack Cocaine Offender Resentencing: An Exploratory Analysis of System Impact.

Gross, S. R., Jacoby, K., Matheson, D. J., Montgomery, N., & Patil, S. (2005). Symposium: Innocence in Capital Sentencing – Exonerations in the United States, 1989 Through 2003. *The Journal of Criminal Law & Criminology*. 95 (2), 523.

Haney, C. (2005). *Death by design: Capital punishment as a social psychological system*. American psychology-law society series. New York: Oxford University Press.

Hangartner, J. (1994). *The Constitutionality of Large Scale Police Tactics: Implications for the Right of Intrastate Travel*. School of Law Pace Law Review. http://digitalcommons.pace.edu/cgi/viewcontent.cgi?article=1355&context=lawrev

Hoeffel, J. (2010, March 25). Bid to put tax on pot makes ballot; Measure to legalize marijuana again puts state at front of the nation's drug debate. *Los Angeles Times*, pp. 1AA

Jensen, E. L., & Gerber, J. (1998). *The new war on drugs: Symbolic politics and criminal justice policy.* ACJS/Anderson monograph series. Highland Heights, KY: Academy of Criminal Justice Sciences.

Marez, C. (2004). *Drug wars: The political economy of narcotics.* Minneapolis: University of Minnesota Press.

Piche, D. M., Ed, Taylor, W. L., Ed, & Reed, R. A., Ed. (2002). *Rights at Risk: Equality in an Age of Terrorism. Report of the Citizens' Commission on Civil Rights.* http://www.cccr.org/RightsAtRisk.htm.

Prenzler, T. (2009). *Police corruption: Preventing misconduct and maintaining integrity.* Boca Raton: CRC Press.

Pratt, T. C. (2009). *Addicted to incarceration: Corrections policy and the politics of misinformation in the United States.* Los Angeles: SAGE.

Punch, M. (2009). *Police corruption: Deviance, accountability and reform in policing.* Devon: Willan Publishing.

Shiner, M. (2009). *Drug use and social change: The distortion of history.* Houndmills, Basingstoke, Hampshire [England]: Palgrave Macmillan.

Sterling, E. E. (2004). Drug Policy: A Challenge of values. *Criminal Justice: Retribution vs. Restoration*. New York: Haworth Press.

VH1! Rock Docs Ep. 119 "NWA" The World's Most Dangerous Group" (Producer). (10/03/08). (TV series). Broadcasting group.

Vick, K. (2009, November 23). Support for legalizing marijuana grows rapidly around U.S.; Approval for medical use expands alongside criticism of prohibition. *The Washington Post*, pp 7A

Appendix C

8:55pm 5·11·16

i couldn't done a couple things different for me to rather came to prison like #1 follow the law and #2 paid a lil more attention to the advice that was given to me throughout my life by multiple people who cared, loved and tried to help a young Black Boy that was obviously lost and going in the wrong direction! now that I'm in prison and have been here for the past 6 years on a ten year sentence i've ajusted ok but at first it was hard! Being 18 years old and fresh off the streets i had a real hard problem with accepting authority and Being told what to do. specially By in my case a guard thats my age or just a couple of years older but clearly less intelegent and obviously on a power trip! or maybe somebody that reminds you of the guy who tried to get picked on in middle school and now seek revenge! sounds funny But thats Been my life for the past 6 years.

If you've never Been to prison its really something hard to imagen. You can Be told over and over and watch the movies But thats honestly not enough! Its hard to explain them Being took away from "everything" feels. friends, family, food, clothes, sunlight, fresh air, Freedom! i mean everything!

261

Some situations are worse than others depending on the weather and your Behavor But to me its all the same. if you aint strong it'll do the worse to your spirit and Brake you all the way down. i done seen people that i knew from the outside that were players, Ballers and gangstas come down here and lose who they was litterally! players was they hair from stress thats coming from all different direction. Ballers that Broke and had everything less than Ballin cuz they done lost all support from the outside world and cant even get to commissery and By a 25¢ soup. and gangstas Gritt you know its Body When this shit got men thinkin that other men starting to look attractive. its sad But true. people kill they self on a daily Basis in here. I seen a man layin dead on the floor not even 10 feet away from me for atleast 10 minutes Before they came and attempted to give him medical attention. its scary just thinkin about the diffrent risk you take just waking up and making it thru the day. from Riots where you got two people (litterally) fighting at on time with shanks metal heart and anything.

else they can Be used as a weapon to throwing & worry about a person that had a Bad day at home and had it on this or her mind to come to work and let it out on the first person they saw. and either you an Inmate in all while your always wrong even when your right! Having to depend on someone who doesn't care about your well Being for protection or help and most times your Biggest threat makes it that much Harder to Be in a good mood or keep a good spirit! most people just fell right In place with the Bullshit, violence and everything else that aint productive. its Hard to Be a leader in a place like this and when i say leader i mean someone who leads his own thoughts and action and not let his situation and serrounding change who him' i can say that im Blessed to Be able to experience this exprience without losing myself But even more learning and finding myself i had to make the choice to change my life By changing my thought process and then my actions. I needed to see first Hand that this aint how i wanted to spend the rest of my life or any extra Years! most importantly is what we choose to to with our time. I exercize my mind By Reading for the most part and now trying understand life to the Best of my

ability. to me its as the death than a reality check!
I see life in a whole new aspect and having everything taken from me slowly made my value the
small things in life that i was taken from for granted
like using the restroom in private, goin outside
when the sun's out or even chewing a piece of gum!
    I don't know how things will Be when i get out
But as for me one thing that i can garentied is that
i will Be more pasient, humble, appreciative and dedicate
to my goals and morals in life. i feel that im ready
to get out and put all my plans into action. i took my
time and used it as preperation so that i'll Be able to
live my life at the fullest potential possible. i dont
look at life just something that i have to do until i
die anymore. i look at life as an opportunity in every
direction. i learned that love realy was at the Background so much hate and that happiness was after
Been sad for so long. long story short i see things for
what they realy are now and By me still Being in
Prison and still learning and By me learning what
i've learned, i'll continue to learn even after im
done doing time Behind prison walls. i
    I trust myself, trust my talents and protected
my craft with the time that i've had to myself.

264

You will find some of the most talented people in prison in almost every category possible. Rappers, Ball players, Book writers, artists... you can name it. I even seen somebody make a light bulb out of simple things like paper clips and paper. Speakers from card board and magnets, tatto guns from screws and wires, pressure cookers, diamonds! In other words sometimes a hard situation will bring out the Best in you and thats called prison this time for me and alot of others who were strong and smart enough to turn a problem into a Blessing.

For any and everybody Having a tough time in life, faced with a problem or just lost and confused. Change is possible! In changing everyday step by step little by little and you can do it. You can do "Anything" Well you put your mind, Body and soul into Regardless how Bad it looks or how much the odds are against you. Keep your Head up, stay Focused and dedicated and make it Happen.

James Mclilen
Aka. Lil Dude

266

Appendix D

Hip Hop in Mainstream Media: The Exploitation and Amplification of Street Life in Hip Hop Culture

Porscha Kelley

Circa 2009

Abstract

For decades, the evasion of inner city delinquencies by local and state government has produced swelling pools of destitute and crime stricken neighborhoods. Within this environment emerged a culture that yearned for a means of expression for its poverty shackled captives. The inhabitants of these neighborhoods cultivated an industrial movement through the utilization of very few resources. The hip hop culture grew in its popularity through three forms; including dance, graffiti, and rap. Hip hop's introduction into the mainstream media made way for a publicized revolutionary movement of otherwise disenfranchised people. Best of all, it gave voice to the entrepreneurial spirit of underrepresented youth.

However, certain conventional conceptions and stereotypical spectacles, coupled with industrialized propaganda have illuminated hip-hop's popular culture in a negative light. Tabloid tactics used in the media tend to glamorize the now overly explicit voice of hip-hop. The presence of this type of behavior in reality has made an impression on what our society views as disruptive occurrences in respect to socially acceptable behaviors. Mediated messages in hip-hop culture have been mirrored in our society to a larger implication, and actions otherwise viewed as highly obscene are now viewed as the norm.

Meager Beginnings

Hip hop in its purest form can be examined in its early stages of development. In the 1970s, a new movement formulated and began to simmer on the streets of Brooklyn, New York. However, the collective culture of hip hop has accumulated as early as the 1930s. During that time, the most popular forms of music consisted of blues and later on a collection of upbeat jazz. The coalition of Jazz and Rock & Roll are considered first cousins of hip hop. The hip hop culture grew in its popularity through three forms including dance, rap, and graffiti. Key turning points in these three forms of expression grew from evolutionary points in past eras of music. The basis for break-dancing had its birth in the legendary cotton club when Earl Tucker incorporated float and slide moves which inspired many of the new age hip hop dance styles. Moves like these were later supported and further encouraged by Clayton Fillyau, a drummer for James Brown, who introduced the break beat; this would later inspire many of the "b-boy movements" performed at block parties in the streets of Brooklyn. Dance has proved to be the staple within the culture of hip hop performance and storytelling (Adaso, 2009).

The second element of hip hop, rap, surfaced through two popular phases. The art of "DJ battling," developed its roots from a 1950 "Soundclash" contest between Coxsone "Downbeat" Dodd and Duke "Trojan" Reid. The influence of rhythmic verse or rap was then widely introduced and made popular by a young boxer named Cassius Clay who, before defeating Sonny Liston, recited one of the earliest rhymes, "Clay comes out to meet Liston And Liston starts to retreat If Liston goes back any further He'll end up in a ringside seat."

The third aspect of hip hop evolved in the crime stricken streets of Harlem and the Bronx where the building of the subway system began and the exodus of affluent whites and Jews occurred at a rapid pace, leaving only poor African Americans and Hispanics. Through artistic expression of shared frustrations, young artists introduced the third element of hip hop by creating murals on subway cars, trains, and semi-demolished buildings. These visuals reflected the injustices experienced within surrounding neighborhoods. The most elaborate of these murals explored images of police brutality, socio-political views, and a mix of territorial gang positions and personal glorification. Over the years, this process converged and a method of tagging gained major popularity. This method expanded and artists began to express their political views from a street perspective on public government funded property. At one point, the act of "tagging," on buildings and subways, led to a $40,000 subway car wash led by the NYC Transit Authority at the Coney Island train yard. To prevent further defacement, cars were sprayed with petroleum hydroxide to minimize the effects of spray paint. These acts of vandalism posed as nuisance to city officials who moved to strictly enforce the law on offenders (Adler, 2004). Hoping to defuse the vandalistic crime, enforcement overlooked the seed of the problem presented in the very "art" they strived to prevent.

Within these three elements lay the foundation of the hip hop culture and form of collective expression. Hip hop had its most raw evolutions during its underground phase. This culture grew from radical groups formed in the mid to late sixties to fight racial injustices. The objectives of groups like the Black Panthers, the Republic of New Africa, and the Revolutionary Action Movement was to establish a visible presence and to voice their views, bringing the needs of the black community to the forefront of the nation's priorities. After the early seventies, these groups disintegrated due to severe legal force, and the remainder of most members formed street gangs. The coalition of these street gangs resulted in some of the most influential groups in early hip hop. One particular end result of these groups originated from the Black Spades street gang. These participates later became known as the Universal Zulu Nation; led by Afrikia Bambaataa. The evolution of street gangs into hip hop crews led to more positive non-violent organized interaction between former gang members of the community. Organizational meetings were present in the form of underground and block parties where crews met and "battled" based on the three pillars of hip hop, dance, rap, and graffiti.

These hip hop parties took place anywhere from the local park to "hole in the wall" areas. More of the park-side parties mostly involved pre-teens, teenagers, and young adults getting together and listening to acts like Kool Herc, Caz, Kurtis Blow and Grandmaster Flash. Building upon the Jamaican tradition of toasting, the emphasis here was a live DJ performer. At these parties, the music and cutting of records was the main attraction where dance crews could show off their skills and battle other neighborhoods on the dance floor. In the late 70s hip hop music turned its attention more toward the MC verses the DJ. As this occurs, more and more live shows by artist like Cold Crush, the Rock Steady Crew, and Casanova Fly are scheduled, advancing the transformation of freestyle rap recorded onto vinyl. As the rap element of hip hop grows in its popularity the growth of counter elements like dance and graffiti follows suit. Noted B-boy groups begin to hit the center stage. In 1978 Charlie Robot, who appeared on "Soul Train" introduced the world to the "Robot" dance (Unknown 2002). Later New York dance crews added shorter movements to their fluid movement and introduced "poppin." Graffiti came to be seen as a visual expression of rap music (Hip Hop: Graffiti).

Introduction to Mainstream Media

Hip Hop's street culture took its first step in becoming a major part of not just American popular culture, but a part of the world's popular culture in 1979. This was accomplished through the introduction of the formal record label and the entry to mainstream media through radio and TV. At the time that the phrase "rap music" was coined, the Sugarhill Gang solidified the structure and visual representative power of the record label within the hip hop community (Adler, 2004). This group represented a unique perspective in a changing environment; within the hip hop street culture, rap crews or groups usually shared a common genuine bond. Groups formed to represent the community—or block—they grew up in or some collective purpose they worked together to achieve. The Sugarhill Gang was hip hop's first commercial hip hop group and because of this many authentic rap groups did not think they truly represented a genuine rap group. Although the Sugarhill Gang was presented to the world as an iconic rap group, the three members of the group were found randomly by record mogul Sylvia Roberts and coaxed together. It has been said that one of the member's verse, Big Bank Hank, of the song "Rapper's Delight" was authored by another rap artist. Big Bank even repeats the original artist's name in the rhyme. He sampled his entire flow from a neighborhood star by the name of Grandmaster Caz. This chain of events set hip hop up in preparation for its second phase of exposure leaving behind its meager beginnings and setting the stage for a mainstream debut into the record selling industry. What was once an intimate neighborhood experience was about to be packaged and sold to the entire country. After Sugarhill's initial chart topping success, other artists began recording their rhymes on vinyl and opening their own record labels. Soon to follow the hit "Rapper's Delight" in 1979, Kurtis Blow released "Christmas Rappin" on Mercury Records, Grandmaster Flash and the Furious Five released "Superrappin" on Enjoy Records, and Jimmy Spicer released "Adventures of Super Rhymes" on Dazz Records. 1980 became the year of the record label battles.

Continuous record play on the radio made way for hip hop's entrance into TV, which provided a much wider avenue in introducing the culture of hip hop to America. On February 14, 1981, The Funky 4 plus One More became the first hip hop group to appear on a national television show, NBC's *Saturday Night Live*. In this same year, ABC's 20/20 aired the first national television coverage of the "Rap Phenomenon". At this point hip hop began to further evolve and traditional hip hop culture started to reach beyond its black and latino ties in New York. The Beastie Boys, a group composed of three white boys from Middle America, formed an iconic band. As the scope of accepted artists began to widen, women began to become major players in the eye of the hip hop community. Disproving the soft and passive characteristics of the average woman's persona, some of the most recognized female MCs approached the stage. Roxanne Shante's mix of the Kango Crew in the song "Roxanne's Revenge" in1984 was one of the first popular exposures that led to the introduction of women as respected equals into the rap game. And in 1985 Salt 'n' Pepa make their first appearance on Super Nature's "The Show Stopper". Other acts were soon to follow that further evolved the female rapper's persona as a reflection from the male MC's perspective.

As hip hop artists began to take center stage their music began to climb official music charts gaining further recognition. The fusion between rap and rock widened the views on hip hop and allowed the room it needed to grow. In 1982, the first international hip hop tour took place in Europe through which major parts of Europe and Asia became exposed to the culture. Artists quickly began to cross over into other venues of entertainment like print and TV ads. After years of being neglected, mainstream media accepts hip hop on a wider basis and introduced MTV's first show to cater to rap and its audience in 1988, *Yo MTV Raps*. This effort could not be achieved without the presence of Michael Jackson who premiered as the first black artist to get air time on MTV ever with his video/short movie "Thriller." Later entire shows would be dedicated to the exploration of hip hop music.

The perks of national attention later led to established artists receiving just due accolades and recognition. The first Grammy was award to a rap artist in 1989 for the best performance by DJ Jazzy Jeff and the Fresh Prince; however momentous the event may have seemed, the salubrious celebration took on a somber mood once it was learned that that the award committee decided to present the award off stage (Adler, 2004). Demanding the respect artists felt they deserved, several high profile hip hop and R&B artist publicly announced their decision to boycott the 1989 Grammy ceremony.

This stint of independence helped artists to further claim their careers and establish themselves separate from their status as marionette puppets of the record label. Hip hop's introduction into the mainstream media made way for a publicized revolutionary movement of otherwise disenfranchised individuals. Best of all, it gave voice to the entrepreneurial spirit of underrepresented youth. The birth of the crossover artist expanded into developing entrepreneurial ventures of their own. Not only did future music moguls release other artists under their own managing-producing labels, but artists like Will Smith and Queen Latifah merged into the TV/Film industry, while others, like RUN DM and LL Cool J, gained major endorsements with apparel companies like Adidas and FUBU.

Tabloid Tactics: A Glamorized Media Frenzy

Channels of media are our primary source of communication in this country. The use of rap in the African American community functions to a certain capacity as a voice that recognizes the black identity, the black experience, and the integrated messages of struggles pertaining to police brutality, drug infestation, a deficient of necessary resources, and government desertion. The commercialism of hip hop further opened the door to hip hop culture through the reflection of these same issues in cinema. Films like *Krush Grove*, produced in 1985, used early music video shooting aspects as an avenue of exploring an otherwise simplistic storyline. On a more influential note, films like *Do the Right Thing*, 1989, featured songs like "Fight the Power," which represented a political rap anthem by Public Enemy that attempted to raise the consciousness of the black community. However more frequently, in black cinema associated with hip hop, we find that the investments in detail and storyline mainly explore the ghettos and the youthful black male actions in coping with the status quo. The existence of the black community, beyond such narrow confines, is ignored. Two of the most successful hip hop films of the past two was

American Gangsta (2007) and *Notorious* (2009), which grossed over $265 million and $42 million in ticket sales respectively. Both these films explore the life of two street entrepreneurs involved in drug distribution and a highly glamorized life.

Later, these entrepreneurial ventures stretched far beyond movie roles into everything from sports drinks endorsements, makeup lines, and biographical video and book productions. The print phenomenon in particular began to expand and gain momentum within the hip hop community. Within the print industry, hip hop cultured magazine and book companies catering to the hungry urban based audience grew. The main stories covered in these print productions revolved around guns, drugs, women, jail time, and highly successful artists with very little education. Print has become one of the main mediums to glamorize otherwise vulgar yet seducing headlining issues in the hip hop community. Infamous criminals and artists are actively able to cash in on their reputations portrayed in print media.

Autobiographical tell-all books began to fly off selves at an astronomical pace. Majority of these recounts centered on the additive life styles of gang banging, drug dealing, and legal bouts. One author, "Monster" Kody Scott found his notoriety as a best-selling author of two books *Monster: The Autobiography of an L.A. Gang Member* and *T.H.U.G. L.I.F.E.* Through the publication of his memoirs, accomplished during one of his jail stays, Scott was launched into the public's eye. When he returned home, he found that his gangster image he tried so hard to shed behind California bars after his conversion to Islam had greatly increased in reverence. "Monster" Kody, now named Sanyika Shakur, gained an unimaginable reputation among younger gang bangers and found that he would forever be confined to this simplistic heartless killer idealized in his books (BET 2008). Instead of depicting the strife and struggle to turn his life around, the recount in Shakur's books set the standard of what gangster life should look like. AS of 2008 a film titled "Can't Stop Won't Stop" is scheduled to further expose the underlying grim dealings of street life in a glamorize fashion. Today Sanyika Shakur serves a life sentence in a California correctional facility after reaching the peak of his gang banger career by being listed as one of the FBI's "Top 10 Most Wanted Gang Members."

Through the years, the growing attraction to the recreation of celebrity's lives and reality television has fast forwarded the speed in which celebs have been able to exploit their involvement with severe legal infractions and street activity. Rapper Clifford "TIP" Harris is among the growing list of celebs that have been able to enter the world of reality television through a circle of controversy. With the ever increasing gun violence crimes appearing in heart wrenching news stories across America, "TIP" Harris appears on prime time news stations facing two felony charges for possession of unregistered machine guns and possession of firearms by a convicted felon. As a part of his sentencing Mr. Harris will have to serve one year and jail in conjunction with completing 1,000 hours of community service. In a valiant effort to use the press of the media to spin the situation and depict himself in a brighter light, he created a reality show titled "T.I.'s Road to Redemption: 45 Days to Go." In this reality "TIP" Harris takes the time to interview six teens whose lives have already been tainted by several juvenile offenses and even more serious violations like breaking and entering with the intent to rob. He then counsels these individuals using his life as an example and employing the true life stories of former gang bangers and drug dealers.

Before "TIP's" entrance onto the stage of reality television, another rapper by the name of Kimberly "Lil Kim" Jones approached the self-promoted publicity stunt of reality shows in 2006. "Lil Kim" was indirectly involved in a shooting outside of a popular night club. Her legal issues surfaced when she took the stand in court and perjured herself to protect the shooter. Ironically, in the end the shooter saved himself by copping to a guilty plea and testifying against "Lil Kim" and others who lied to protect his guiltiness. "Lil Kim" was ultimately charged with refusing to cooperate with a criminal investigation and sentenced to one year in prison. The self-proclaimed Barbie doll "Lil Kim" chronicled her prolonged trip to prison in the reality show "Lil Kim's Count Down to Lock Down." Through this show, she gained a further following by highlighting her use of the "no snitching" rule of thumb.

The "no snitching" movement stands as an unwritten code of the streets; heavily embraced by the hip hop culture. "No snitching" means not to tell or disperse any useful information to any authoritative figure, especially the police. This movement has cultivated and structured the rule of what it takes to practice true "gangsta-ism" and a commitment to the streets. However, in actuality, this code of conduct has resulted in thousands of unsolved crimes as a result of local police departments' inability to drum up cooperating witnesses. In an effort to reach out into the streets, Reverend Jessie Jackson has worked hard to combat this disastrous ill prioritized rule of the hip hop culture to introduce the "start snitching movement." He hopes to encourage knowledgeable witnesses to step up and take responsibility for helping the victims of their neighborhood.

But as times progresses the growing crime, concentrated in urban areas, has been the prostitution of young girls. Even though these girls are being abused and used for their bodies neither they; nor others within the community, will give up the individuals leading these prostitution rings. The degradation of black women on the street seems to reflect an eerie image of the stereotypical sex object black women in America have been depicted to be. This image has made its way back to into the forefront of reality television, especially prevalent in VH1's presentation of "Flavor of Love." This show exaggerates the representation of the oversexed attitudes and presence of members of the African American community. A rap veteran by the name of Flavor Flav documented his search of love by opening up his house to over fifteen women, majority black, who all live with him. In the mist of ridiculous challenges like cleaning trashed hotels and houses, the girls take their turn hoping in and out of bed with Flavor Flav proving their love by how far they will go in the bedroom. As of the early 90's, hip hop music artists have featured sexy women in their videos and how easy it is to get them into the bedroom. It is said that "music and sex have always been kissing cousins," but hip hop music takes it to another level. Within the walls of hip hop, media outlets such as video and film have been used to expose the position of black women not only in hip hop but in the working world. This is done through the vehicle of raps smutty lyrics or raunchy rhetoric elicit graphic videos, cable television shows, and hip hop themed magazines. Hip hop further perpetuates the disrespect of the position of women in the world of the man. Although hip hop, alone, cannot be the blame, countless other American ventures of exploiting woman have prospered, i.e. play boy, and been counted as being less vulgar than that of the hip hop culture.

This depiction of women as nothing more than sexual objects has culminated a wider effect on young women's behavior and their ideas about body images reflected in videos, print ads, and magazines. The prostitution of young women has grown and their attitude towards this practice has grown very loose, as you see more women on stage and in videos imitating strippers and hip-hop "models." An example, such as the highly acclaimed video girl Melissa Ford has made a more than fine living for herself as an object for the last six or so years. At first glance, the average professional would not guess that this sexy video vixen holds a Bachelor's and Master's degree in Psychology. One would ask the question, "Why does she choose to do what she does as such an educated woman? She has been quoted saying that she makes a really good living at what she does. In reality Ms. Ford is only a few of the ones that do make a more than descent living as a video "model." Video girls are seen as less than. Some of the women begin as extras in videos and regularly receive little to no pay; it is done for attention and in hopes of getting paid well at some point.

Besides degrading lyrics, the hip hop culture in the print media in particular, has proven itself more destructive than constant videos. "The line that once divided pop culture from porn culture continues to be blurred. On one side of the line are [sic] the making of sexually explicit materials who fashion their operations, marketing practices, and star system after Hollywood (Watkins)." This is utterly apparent in today's evolved hip hop culture. Porn has become increasingly visible in mainstream television, film, music, and advertising, even outside of the bounds of the hip hop culture, in mainstream media period.

Press Play in Reality

The depiction and demonization of the African American community in film, TV, and other avenues of the media have long been discussed, documented, and used to promote stereotypes. As time has passed, hip hop culture has reverted back to these old images and has been compared to menstrual shows. The over glamorized presence and influence of drugs, guns, and violence has shown itself in the real world. Through tabloid like tactics utilized by the media, artists' notability has been diverted from the emphasis on lyrical skills to novelty and popularity based on publicity stunts including street violence and the accrual of street credit. These attributes of the hip hop game have directly contributed to materialism, financial incompetency, poor views on formal education, and gang violence within the urban community.

Media has proven itself as a very important tool in shaping our interpretations, expectations, and what we perceive to be reality. Hip hop spread throughout the streets of New York through word of mouth and true to life contact, but its introduction into popular culture occurred through radio and television. In this instance, mass media could and has been used as a tool in maintaining ideological hegemony within our society (Berry 1996).

The media took the voice of hip hop and its message and distorted it and minimized its consciousness. The media's role in this practice was to form a distinct ideology using the fabrication of images and the process of representation to persuade the viewer that things are how they ought to be, with the hip hop African American culture at the bottom of this sophisticated hierarchy of classes. This projects the basis of the hip hop community in a negative light. Images perpetuated in the media has steered perceptions of hip hop and has in turn presented a certain overly imaginative violent atmosphere leading to a convoluted state of hip hop culture. Hip hop's reputation in the media serves as a "gerrymandered framework producing and naturalizing racial representations (Berry 1996)." In the African American history, stereotypical ideals and attributes have been formed, nationalized, and solidified over decades. These stereotypes become ideologies and norms within the American culture and are farther exaggerated in the hip hop world portrayed in the hip hop mainstream culture.

Several occurrences have reflected this type of acceptable framing. On April 4, 2007 a white radio host, Don Imus, commentated on a college women's basketball game. One of the teams happened to be the Rutger's women's team, whom consisted of 11 African American women between the ages of 18-22. As Imus commentated on a particular play, he replied that "that's some nappy headed hoes" (Wikipedia 2009). This comment not only played into long standing stereotypes of black women having untamable hair compared to the white woman; but it reverted back to days of slavery when a black women could do nothing else but serve as an unwed bedmate to their white master. This comment also insulted the young women on the team by degrading their efforts as college educated women athletes. They were reduced in one phrase from being smart, articulate, hardworking athletes; to nothing but unattractive sexual objects. In Imus' defense, he used the use of the word "hoe" in hip hop verses to validate his right to also express the same feeling about African American women.

This type of sexual reflection in our society has been worse. In 1998, the outplay of a scene of unity and pride turned into a disaster where several people were trampled and injured, young women were stripped of their clothes, molested, and sprayed in the face with alcohol and water. At the Puerto Rican parade in Florida black and Puerto Rican males of the crowd cheered in laughter while inappropriately groping female members of the audience. The horrified faces of the women along with their screams went unanswered. This scene depicted the presence of a current hip hop video in the streets of any "hood."

The disrespect of women displayed in the hip hop culture is portrayed as real and as what artists' see and experience. In videos and lyrics, artists refer to women as whores, sexual objects, prostitutes, welfare queens or gold diggers that are looking for the next rap star. As the repetition of these images penetrate mainstream media, these stereotypes solidify and work as real world ideology and not just ideas in this fantasy world created by oversexed artists in a ghetto setting full of diamonds, platinum, and champagne.

These effects have a clear correlation between the transformations in the hip hop culture and the areas in the U.S. where this culture is dominate. Hip hop grew from a pool of crime and violence. Artists found fame and fortune by actively drawing attention to injustices and unfair chances at life, but now it is ignored and covered by the glamorization of the life they escaped through exploitation. Yet some artists never fully escaped their impoverished life style even though their bank account reflected the contrary. The realistic implications and outcome of this crime is minimized in the minds of those who watch from the outside looking in. Those audience members, who have expansive exposure to this type of behavior, absorb this lifestyle through the media (Rome 2004).

The question still remains, does the majority of these problems exist because of the images projected in the media that glorify certain types of actions in hip hop culture influence certain actions? Or, does hip hop portrayed in the media only reflect an already prevalent culture and expose it on a higher level of reception? Glamorized tabloid tactics are used in an attempt to sell more records, continue growing stereotype—or to prove old ones—and try to maintain a shocking appeal to audience. These actions are double-sided swords used by the artists, the industry, and those who have influence on mainstream media, all for their own interest. But, the issue arises when these tactics begin to influence communities in a negative manner.

References

C. Watkins. (2005). *Hip Hop Matters*. Boston: Beacon Press

H. Adaso. (2009). "Hip-Hop Timeline: 1925-2007 The History of Hip Hop Music". Retrieved January 11, 2009, from About.com Web site: http://rap.about.com/od/hiphop101/a/hiphoptimeline.htm

Unknown. (2002). "Unofficial Hip Hop Timeline". Retrieved January 14, from B-Boys.com Web site: http://www.b-boys.com/classic/hiphoptimeline.html

"Hip Hop: Graffiti". (n.d.). Rretrieved March 16, 2009, from Wikipedia: http://en.wikipedia.org/wiki/Hip_hop

Documentary: B. Adler. (2004) *And You Don't Stop: 30 Years of Hip Hop*. VH1 Classic Roc Docs.

Documentary: (2008) American Gangster: Monster Kody. BET.

S. Reid. (2009). "T.I. Counts Down To Prision Sentence In MTV Series." Retrieved April 1, 2009 from MTV Web site: http://www.mtv.com/news/articles/1602819/20090115/t_i_.jhtml

V. Berry, C. Manning-Miller. (1996). Mediated *Messages and African-American Culture: Contemporary Issue*. Thousand Oaks: Sage.

"Don Imus: Rutgers Women's Basketball Controversy. (n.d.). Retrieved February 28, 2009 from http://en.wikipedia.org/wiki/Don_Imus#Rutgers_women.27s_basketball_controversy

D. Rome. (2004). Black Demons: The Media's Depiction of the African American Male Criminal Stereotype. Westport, Conn.: Praeger.

Made in the USA
Columbia, SC
06 January 2023

74144026R00154